January, 1992

To Martha & Larry,

I so enjoyed meeting you.
May you continue to enjoy your
own gift of time.

Warmest wishes,
Beverly

A Gift of Time

A collection of essays
by Beverly Beckham

Photography
by Beth Erickson

Host Creative Communications
Lexington, Kentucky

"A Gift of Time" is published and printed by Host Creative Communications, 904 North Broadway, Lexington, Kentucky 40505.

Edited by Ed Kromer
Designed by Michaela Ristich Duzyk

ISBN: 1-879688-00-X

Essays are reprinted with permission from *The Boston Herald* and *The Patriot Ledger*. Photographs originally appeared in *The Canton Journal* and *The Canton Citizen*.

 This book is printed on recyclable paper.

*To my husband, Bruce, whose belief in me
has never wavered*

Contents

Winter

Spring

Preface

I t is noon and I am riding my bike, pedaling in and out of shadows, up and down streets, past gardens and lawns and a field that's just been cut; past a horse and two cows sprawled lazily under a tree.

I am pedaling hard up a hill, past a country club, deserted this day. Then I coast — past a furniture store with chaise lounges in the window, past a nursery full of petunias and geraniums, past a busy market and an empty church. The shadows grow scarce, the traffic next to me spitting up dust and pebbles, sucking the sweetness out of the air, tinging it with exhaust. I am pedaling steadily now, the shadows gone, the sun hot, intense, like a space heater left on high.

It is then that it happens. In the heat and in the macadam, in the dirt sprayed up from the road, in the bray of cars and the brightness of the day, in the scent of sand and grass and sweat, in the spotlight of the noon sun, there is suddenly, overpoweringly, not just the memory of another summer day, not just the taste and feel and smell of it, but the day itself, a moment out of time.

That's how it happens. I am doing one thing and the past appears, sometimes as a still photo, sometimes as moving film. Not whole days, not even complete hours, just teasers. I grab on to the teasers. I inspect them, superimpose them on today, compare and contrast.

"Where do you get your ideas?" people ask. I don't get them. They get me.

Earlier this year, I was in Maine, walking along the wide, smooth beach I walk along every spring. Only this year the beach was littered with pebbles and boulders, where before there had been only sand.

Our memories are like rocks deposited at the ocean's edge, unearthed by powers over which we have no control, swept into our consciousness randomly, haphazardly. The churning mind is a churning ocean, wearing down days, breaking up moments, rearranging, realigning, reinventing. Entire days, entire years, whole memories are inaccessible because they are buried in a vast and deep sea. But occasionally, pieces break off and are carried to the surface.

The essays and photographs included in this collection are small pieces of the past, universal moments — the first day of school, Christmas morning, Valentines Day, first love, a child's growing up, old age. The feelings are universal, too: love, hope, joy, fear, wonder, despair, renewal, awe.

I wrote these essays over a period of 11 years. During those same 11 years Beth Erickson was capturing different memories and different faces on film. The essays and photographs are about specific people and specific times, separated for this collection into seasons of the year, seasons of our lives.

But they are, in truth, timeless and about us all.

Beverly Beckham

 Spring

A Gift of Time

Give Time," the letter suggested. "Time is the ideal gift."
Would that we could give time. Not the magazine, but the real thing. All wrapped up and held together by a shiny red bow. Happy birthday, Dad. These are the days of your life. Open the package and you're young again, kissing your mother goodbye, hurrying out the door, rushing to school, eager for life.

Fantasy. Pure conjecture, this giving time, yet wonderful to consider.

If I could, I would collect time, pack years in a box for a daughter whose adolescence weighs upon her, who looks in a mirror aching to see Christie Brinkley and sees just herself: too plain, too big, too everything. She would remove the cover from her gift, peek inside and discover the woman she will be, the beauty I already see — tall, bright, witty, delightful. A girl to be proud of. And she would smile, adolescence by-passed. And be content with who she is.

If I could, I would save time for my son, gather yesterday and today and pack them away tenderly so that years from now, when he is a man and encumbered by a man's responsibilities, he would be able to live again two days when life's biggest problem was where to play baseball.

I would freeze time for my youngest daughter, stop the days from marching past, not for her sake — she's eager to grow — but for mine. I don't want her to be too big for my lap. I don't want her to realize I'm not perfect. I don't want her telling me she's old enough to wait alone for the bus, and to please not embarrass her in front of her friends. I want her to like being with me forever. As she does now.

Want to skip school today? Go to Nantasket? The older kids say no, what are you, crazy? It's freezing out. The youngest runs upstairs to find her pail and mittens.

We sip cocoa on the deserted beach. We search for sea glass and chase sea gulls. "I wish I could fly," she whispers dreamily. "I'd fly all over the world and come back with my bucket full of sea glass." "You might fly away forever," I say. "No, Mommy," she promises, hugging me. "I'd never leave you or Teddy."

Time. I'd give a huge package full of healthy weeks and happy days to my mother-in-law, 74 on the outside, 37 inside, my friend, my confidant. Thousands of days. That she may live forever. That we may grow old together.

I'd give years back to my mother. Months spent unconscious, seasons when she was unaware of changes around her. A dozen lost Christmases and birthdays and family celebrations. I would watch as she opened the package with fingers that are twisted and stiff, tiring from the effort. The box would open and a light, like vapor, would escape and magically she would change, her fingers growing strong and straight, her legs limber, the wheelchair gone.

The clock would be ticking and she would see her grandchildren growing younger. She would be back in her old house, in the old neighborhood, and the hi-fi would be on and she would be singing with Mary Martin, and there would be laughter and my father would be smiling and there would be no more hospitals and doctors and nurses.

Then it would be my father's turn and he would open his gift and inside would be a spring night, rich with the smell of new life. And he would recognize the night and hurry to his mother's house and warn her, "Don't smoke when you're tired, Ma, and never when you're in bed." And she would see the concern in his eyes and put out the cigarette and be alive in the morning.

All the limitless possibilities. A gift of time could erase all the errors, undo all the mistakes. There would be no Hitler, no Hiroshima, no assassinations, no Kent States.

Instead we'd have the privilege of playing again and again, like a favorite record, all the good times. Our first movie, our first kiss, our first dance.

And the dance could go on forever.

Soothing Voices from the Past

A soft, young voice fills the living room with hesitant, quaking notes. The old, black 78 spins swiftly, frenetically, conjuring up an image transfixed in time.

"Are you nervous?" the woman asks, clutching the child's hand.

"No, Mama," the girl lies, biting her lip.

"You shouldn't be," she soothes. "You know all the words."

"But you're going first, right?"

"Right," the mother says, squeezing the child's hand and smiling.

Both mother and daughter have come to Boston to a recording studio to cut a record for the man whose life they share. It is to be an anniversary gift, a surprise planned for months. A man with skin creased like corduroy approaches the pair. "It's your turn," he announces cheerfully, leading the way into a room as bright as foil. The child squints and follows him to a seat in the corner. The mother, tall, thin, trembling, hurries to where a microphone sways from the ceiling. She shuffles from one foot to the other. She plays with the red, plastic beads around her neck. She fiddles with her hair and adjusts the folds in her blue serge skirt.

"You're going to have to stand still if you want this to work," an anonymous voice snaps. The child looks around for the voice's owner and locates him, a portly man wearing headphones and a dour expression standing behind a glass wall. A cigarette is pinched between lips that seem stitched into a sneer. The child tries not to look at him or at the nicer man beside her or at her mother. The room is too bright and she doesn't want to sing and she won't remember the words and what if she cries? She bites her lip harder and wishes she were home.

But then sound softens the room, her mother's sound, the thick, husky voice she has heard drifting down the hall from the kitchen into her bedroom for as long as she can remember. The sound soothes and comforts her and makes her forget the bright lights and her own fears and the mean man.

"Why this feeling, why this glow, why the thrill when you say 'Hello?' It's a strange and tender magic you do. Mr. Wonderful, that's you."

"Sing for me, Dorothy," her father says sometimes, late at night when he comes in from work, when she pretends to be sleeping. "I always feel better when I hear you sing."

Her mother has told her that before she was married she had sung "Paper Moon" in a talent show and won first prize. Now she sings in minstrel shows and in the shower and late at night. But to the child, her mother's voice IS the prize, the thing that transforms the ordinary into something magical.

* * *

The child sits on an old wooden chair and memorizes the scene. She is storing it beside the months of preparation that went into making this day possible, recalling the afternoons they'd rolled nickels and dimes, remembering her mother's disappointment when she'd learned that a piano player cost an extra $10.

"I guess I'll have to sing without it," she had sighed.

The child knew it wouldn't matter. Her mother didn't need accompaniment. She always sang alone or to the scratchy tunes that played on the old Victrola, her voice the perfect instrument.

Now it is perfect and full and rich, flooding the room with

strong, confident notes, turning a song into a prayer. When the last note is sung, the child looks at the man in the glass booth and sees tears in his eyes.

The child sings her song without incident. Afterward, they leave the studio together, the mother clutching the record in one hand and her daughter in the other. It is a long way home, by bus and by train. The woman hopes she will not be late, for the recording is to be a surprise.

And it is. On their anniversary, when he listens to the familiar tune, tears cloud the husband's eyes. The old Victrola plays constantly, the tinny tone filling the small apartment, the notes spilling down onto the city street.

* * *

Years later the recording is still cherished. It isn't played as often because it is worn and scratched, because the notes wobble, because it hurts to remember happier times. Still, when I take it from its wrapper, when the music fills the room, my mother's voice — young, soft and sincere — transcends time, filling me with peace and pride and an ache that hurts, but that soothes, too, because it makes me remember its source.

The Boy My Father Used to Be

It was the summer of 1957 when I discovered the boy my father used to be.

I can feel the sun's tinny brightness even now and smell the scent of heat and grass and August indolence that drifted in through the open window as I sat on my mother's bed and studied the letters I'd found in her dresser drawer.

Before that day I thought my father was just like my friends' fathers. He did all the things every father does. He took me to movies; he taught me how to ride a two-wheeler; he held my hand through a succession of polio shots; he bought me sundaes, not just ice cream cones, at the Dairy Queen. He defended me and protected me and even convinced my mother that I should have my own puppy.

Yet as much as I loved him, as close as we were, I never really saw him as anything but a father. His existence began and ended within the confines of our house. What he did away from there was a mystery, like transubstantiation. It was something I accepted but never understood. Until I read the letters.

I found them in a cigar box — El Producto Blunts — hidden under a pile of photographs. I didn't hesitate before opening them. I was allowed to look in that drawer so it didn't occur to me that the letters might be personal. Besides, I knew everything there was to know about my parents. Or so I believed.

But what I discovered in that pile of yellowed letters, in impeccable Palmer penmanship, were the yearnings of someone I didn't know. I found poetry, oh it was grand, and letters describing the hot African desert, days of endless marching and nights spent crouching in a trench.

I knew my father had served in the war, but I knew it the way a 10-year-old knows about life — from images seen on a

19

movie screen, from Audie Murphy heroics in "To Hell and Back." But what I'd seen and what I'd imagined were nothing like the letters I held in my hand. These were filled with "somedays" and "when the war is over" and "I can't wait to be home." They were brooding and sad and impatient.

And so, on that golden afternoon while the neighborhood children screamed that the ice cream man had come, I discovered a little of the boy my father was those distant years before.

> *Because of you my heart is so blue,*
> *Because to me your love was not true.*
> *You left without even a goodbye*
> *And in my heart there is only a sigh.*
>
> *I thought while in a foreign land,*
> *A place where no one understands*
> *That I could always turn to you.*
> *But as this is gone, dear,*
> *We are through.*

I remember only these stanzas but the revelation remains, even now, a profound sense of wonder at having discovered that my father, the gentle, confident man I loved, had been so vulnerable.

I tucked "Because of You" in my pocket and replaced the remaining letters in the drawer. I had a plan.

In the back pages of *Photoplay* and *Modern Screen,* and all the other movie magazines to which I was addicted, were dozens of record companies advertising for quality literature. "We'll put your poem to music," Crown Publishing promised. So I copied the poem on clean, white paper, signed my name and mailed it. A few weeks later, a letter arrived addressed to me.

"Congratulations!" it began. "Your poem 'Because of You' has met our high standards and is qualified to become a song. Just send $75 immediately and we'll set your poem to music."

Seventy-five dollars. It may as well have been a million.

I sold my comic book collection — I had every Little Lulu ever printed — and made five dollars. With my best friend Rose, I put on a neighborhood talent show. We netted $3.20 on that. A lemonade stand brought in $2.40. After three weeks of non-stop effort, I was still $64 short.

"What should I do?" I asked Rose.

"You should tell your father," she said.

When I showed him the letter and my copy of his poem, his mood darkened. But his momentary anger was replaced by something I didn't recognize then but do now: a combination of reverie and regret, the look a man gets when he sees something in himself that he'd forgotten existed.

My father sat at the kitchen table, the poem in his hand, silent for what seemed like forever.

"I appreciate what you were trying to do," he said finally, staring straight into my soul. "But this is the kind of letter these big companies send out to everyone. This poem isn't any good, honey. It never was." Then he sighed.

My father knew everything. He knew how to cut the lawn in broad, even strips. He knew how to get rid of maggots in the garbage. He knew how to fix the TV and the toaster. But he didn't know about this.

"You're wrong, Dad," I said. "That poem deserves to be published. It's wonderful."

"No it isn't honey. It's not special at all."

It was special. It still is. For though in time, I forgot about "Because of You" and gave up trying to get it published, I never forgot what its contents let me glimpse: a shadow of the boy my father used to be before he was my father.

That knowledge has been a treasure, a sweet secret that has forever altered my perception of him and strengthened my love.

Lasting Friendships

Janet lived, not directly across the street, but behind the house across the street. If I looked out my dining room window I could see right into Janet's kitchen.

Despite our proximity, we weren't exactly best friends. It's a wonder we were friends at all. Our beginnings were hardly auspicious.

Second grade. Mid-February. My first day at Tower Hill School. Everyone knew everyone else. Except me. I was the new girl. "Say hello to the new girl," Miss Nagel told the class. Everyone said hello.

I hurried to my seat and slouched down. Within minutes, I started to cry.

"Miss Nagel, Miss Nagel, the new girl is crying," a small child with brownish-red hair in a Brownie uniform shouted. The whole class stared at me.

Janet was the one who told. I swore I would never be her friend.

A week later she knocked on my door. "Wanna go for a walk?" she asked. We hiked to the back of Lewis Drive where freshly poured foundations stood in the shadow of great mountains of dirt waiting to be leveled. No houses were in sight. We could have been the only two people on earth.

"Let's climb to the top," Janet said. I did, while she watched.

"Come on," I shouted from the top of the world. "Come up here!"

"I can't," Janet screamed. "There are snakes all through that dirt. Millions of them, crawling everywhere! Don't move. I'll go get help."

Terrified, I stood immobile, mumbling Hail Marys, praying for her to come back.

More than an hour later, after eating lunch and watching

Candlepin bowling, she returned.

"You can come down now," she said, her voice rich with authority. "The snakes are gone."

Trembling, brushing away tears, I crept down the hill. Of course there were no snakes. But I didn't know that. I thanked Janet for saving my life.

Thirty years later, we laugh at this memory.

Thirty years.

We don't live near each other anymore. Three thousand miles separate us. We don't go exploring together, or sit on the front steps on hot summer nights, weaving tales of beautiful maidens outwitting scurrilous foes, scratching mosquito bites, planning our lives.

We don't play jacks in my kitchen and marbles in her driveway or skip down Chesnut Street singing "Felix the Cat" on the way to St. Bernadette's. We haven't watched "Fury" in decades and most of the places where we played no longer exist. We are adults and intervals of years separate our visits.

Yet nothing has changed. I never see her or think about her without picturing a child in a Brownie uniform, waving her hand furiously. I never remember her without being thankful for her presence in my life.

Janet flew home last week to visit her parents and I knocked on a door I'd pushed open at least a million times and entered the house where I spent so much of my childhood. And for the time I was there I felt safe again.

We sat in the living room — the same room where we watched Audie Murphy movies on Sunday afternoons, and talked about the past. Once we had spent hours there talking only of the future. What bound us then were dreams; what binds us now are memories.

Our friendship is rich with memories. Planted in the soil of

Davis Road and Chesnut Street, it was nurtured by thousands of hours of conversation, hundreds of nights sleeping over, sharing secrets. We fed it with honesty, that lack of artifice that exists only when you're young and have nothing to hide. And it grew, through the years, strong and hardy.

There were times we ignored it; times we took off with other friends and forgot each other. We attended different high schools. Life interfered. We tested our friendship, pulled at it, ached to be free of a relationship that couldn't endure anything less than the truth. We were growing up. There were things we wanted to hide.

But the roots of our friendship were strong. They looked on tempests and were never shaken. And the friendship endured. And endures still. Thirty years and 3,000 miles simply do not exist.

Janet walks into a room and we pick up in mid-sentence as if she's been gone only a minute to answer a door, not four years living a life.

"Once upon a time there was a beautiful princess," all our stories began. And they would go on and on into the night, stories that had no limits, stories that matched our dreams.

"Once upon a time," we say now and time coalesces. Yesterday becomes today. And the entire drama that was our childhood is real, like a 3-D movie where the hero is close, so close, you can almost touch him and hold on, for just a second.

That's how it is. That's how it was. That's how it will be. Always.

It Goes So Fast

If God wanted to give mothers the perfect Mother's Day gift, he would start stamping freshly made bottoms with a surgeon general-type warning: "Caution: This child is on loan. Raising him or her may be hazardous to your heart."

It's not as good as a rebate or a 10-day money-back guarantee, but these few indelible words of warning would spare mothers a lot of heartache. Then these tiny people wouldn't trick you with their toothless smiles and precious little gurgles. Every time you changed them you'd read the warning and somewhere inside, the words would be absorbed and your heart would toughen up a little and wouldn't be so susceptible to breakage when, years later, the little guy who said "I'll never leave you, Mommy," forgets to send a card on Mother's Day.

Just a warning, you know?

"Small children, small heartaches. Big children, big heartaches," my grandmother used to say, staring at a picture of a son she hadn't seen in years.

I was young, my child a baby, so I smiled and said, "I know, Nana. I understand." But I didn't. I didn't know about letting go, about being content with a phone call on holidays, about raising a child to give him away to the world. My son was in my arms, not on the other side of the country. So I wasn't worried. I had read the experts. They had the answers. I'd follow their advice and my children would grow up and I wouldn't grieve when my job was done. I'd be prepared. I didn't need any visible warning.

In the beginning it was so easy being a mother. My son slept through the night, seldom fussed and never cried. "You're lucky to have such a good baby," people said. And I smiled and murmured a polite, "Thank you." But I didn't think his being good had anything to do with luck. It had to do with skilled mothering. I had a good baby because I'd read Spock and Bettelheim. Of course my baby would be good. Was there ever any doubt?

I painted baseboards while he sat in an infant seat and watched. I took him to the movies and he would drink his bottle and fall asleep in my lap. I dressed him up and wheeled him around shopping malls where strangers would stop and say, "Isn't he a handsome, adorable boy." And I would bask in the praise, believing I had hand-crafted him, believing he was truly mine.

Then along came Baby Number Two. Maybe I forgot to read the fine print in Spock, because for the first six months of this child's life, she screamed constantly. I bought updated psychology books. I called the pediatrician. I talked to sympathetic friends. I walked, rocked, paced, pleaded, but nothing worked. To get her quiet, I'd have to put on her snowsuit, strap her in the car seat and drive around town. She liked cars. She liked listening to Don McLean's "American Pie." The music and the motion lulled her to sleep. But when the car eased into the driveway and the music died, she pursed her tiny lips and bellowed even louder.

Her screaming made me think that maybe I didn't have as much control as I thought; maybe I didn't have all the answers. So I bought more books. I believed in written-down solutions for every problem. I expected guidance and guidelines. But I found no easy formula, no "right" way to raise a child. I was searching for a never-fail recipe: Combine one infant, one mother and father, mix two cups of love, a cup and a half of understanding and a stick of patience. Fold in trust and perseverance. Add enough tears and laughter to hold the mixture together and bake in moderate oven for 18 years.

Would that it worked this way. But it doesn't. The books

don't have all the answers. Nothing prepares you for the sad fact that even when you succeed as a parent, even when you make it past all the stumbling blocks — "Why can't I ride my bike to the store?" "What do you mean I can't go to the party?" "I absolutely refuse to wear braces!" "Why can't I stay out all night?" Even when you've raised a healthy, happy, well-adjusted child, you don't always win. Because when the mothering is done, when the job is finished, the child leaves. He kisses you goodbye and promises to call. And that's it.

It doesn't seem fair somehow, all the mothers sitting at home waiting to be remembered. A mother and child start out as one. At birth the physical connection is replaced with an emotional one as strong and as essential as the umbilical cord.

All those beginning years, all the time when the children are babies, mutual love passes like electricity, back and forth along that cord. The baby cries and you pick him up and he hugs you, and you smell his baby smell and he feels your arms protecting him and it's reassuring for both of you.

All the time they're growing, they hurry home from school to show you the picture they drew. And the reward of mothering is that picture, taped to the refrigerator; the dandelion plucked from the yard by chubby fingers; the card that says, "To the best mother in the world."

But the cord breaks. It's natural, this growing up, this growing apart. The ties beg to be broken. But it hurts because when it happens you realize what you should have always known: your children were not designed by you and were never really yours. They're visitors who occupy your body, your house, your heart and your mind. The most you can hope is that they'll visit sometime. The most you can hope is that they won't forget you.

A Valentines Heart — Breaker

On Valentines Day in fifth grade, Miss Nagel opened her school bag and pulled from it a huge milk chocolate Russell Stover heart, hollow, yes, but with an embossed cupid right in the middle. Immediately after the Pledge of Allegiance, she held up that heart, promising that after lunch, during our Valentine party, she was going to write a number on a piece of paper. Whoever guessed that number would take the heart home.

I looked for signs all morning. We had math and I counted the number that came out most often in my answers. I counted the buttons on Janet Butler's clothes, then the punches in my conduct card. (Miss Nagel would take a paper puncher and make a hole in an index card each of us had, every time she caught us talking. I talked a lot, so I had more holes than most.)

At recess, I counted the posts in the fence in the schoolyard, the number of people in groups, then counted how many steps there were back up the stairs to our classroom.

"What number are you going to pick?" Janet whispered in the middle of silent reading. I added the numbers of the page I was on and told her I was thinking of picking that.

"Are you talking again?" Miss Nagel suddenly boomed from the front of the class. She had great ears, that woman. Two little syllables and she was beside me, puncher in hand, clicking away.

After lunch, the party finally began and all the Valentine cards that we had written at home and deposited in a box decorated with white doilies and pink hearts were sorted and delivered to us. I didn't count the cards because we all received the same number. "Be sure to include everyone, boys and girls," Miss Nagel had said. We did, but cleverly saved the Valentines with the ugly dogs and the "This is no TAIL" verses for the people we didn't like at all.

In the middle of the party, right out of the blue, George Falcone walked by my desk and slipped me a pink candy heart that said "Be Mine." I turned to him to make sure this was real and he smiled. A few minutes later I found his card in my pile. A big card with a fuzzy red heart on the front. A pretty card with a sentimental verse inside. A special card, signed not in pencil but in ink that would last forever, LOVE, GEORGE.

Love, George? First "Be Mine." Then a smile. Then "Love, George." George Falcone was the cutest boy in the whole fifth grade, the cutest boy in the world! And he loved me. That's what he wrote. Love, George.

"Look at what George Falcone gave me," I said to Janet Butler who took the card, looked at it, then rifled through her pile of cards and produced an exact one of her own. There was the fuzzy red heart on the front. There was the sentimental verse. And there, horror of horrors, was the same signed-in-ink declaration: Love, George.

"It's time to take your seats for the winning of the heart," Miss Nagel said. We sat. She wrote down a number, then one by one, around the room, we guessed at it.

When it was my turn, I said seven, not because there are seven letters in the name Falcone, but because Bobby Fletcher, who sat beside me, told me he was absolutely positive he had seen Miss Nagel write the number seven. How he could have seen this from half a room away when the kids at the front of the room who had guessed and guessed wrong, hadn't seen, I didn't know. But I said seven anyway, because it was as good a number as any.

I actually won the heart, the only thing I've ever won in

my life. George Falcone sidled up to me while Janet and I were waiting in line for the bus. "Aren't you going to give me a piece of your heart?" he asked.

I was 11 and didn't have the words to tell him I already had. So I did the next best thing: I opened the box, split the heart in two, took the bigger piece for myself, and Janet and I ate the whole thing in front of him.

The Bills Can Wait

"Mommy, will you play cards with me?"

It is 7:50 in the morning. The older children have just left for school. I am drinking coffee and reading the newspaper. I do not feel like playing cards. "I'll play in a little while," I say, hoping she'll become distracted by something else.

"I'll shuffle the cards while I'm waiting," she announces, skipping out to the family room.

A few minutes later, I begin to clear the kitchen table.

"Mommy, you promised you'd play with me."

Trapped, I pour myself another cup of coffee and settle down on the family room floor.

"Okay. What do you want to play? Fish?"

"No. I don't like Fish. I want to play War."

In an instant, I see my morning disappear like the steam from my coffee cup. War is an interminable, boring game.

"But Julie," I moan, "I have a zillion things to do. I have to —"

"Please, Mommy?"

I look at my daughter, her eyes like blue buttons, her ponytails awry, her last-year's bathrobe too small, offering me the cards hopefully. And I see myself, years ago, pleading with my father, "Please, Dad, please play War with me?"

I would corner him when he walked through the door early in the morning after working all night. I was bright-eyed and cheery, a night's sleep behind me. He was weary and worn, yearning for rest. But he always played with me.

War was my favorite card game because it lasted forever and because my father never intentionally lost. He was the General Patton of the spades, hearts, clubs and diamonds. A challenge was never to be ignored. And if he pretended, all those years, to like playing and winning for my sake, he did a fine job. He never said, "I'm too tired to play" or "Gee, I don't have the time right now" or "I have a zillion things to do." War, to him, was never boring. "War is war," he would wink. "And may the better man win."

"Okay," I relent, burdened by my memories. "Let's play. I'm going to beat you."

She gives me a hug and carefully deals out the cards.

An hour passes. I call a temporary truce.

"Just let me do the dishes and then I'll finish, all right?"

"Do you promise you'll finish?" she asks, reluctant to let me go.

I promise and linger over the sink trying to devise a way to lose.

If I don't lose soon, the house will not get cleaned, the bills will not be paid and I will never get to the library.

Still, I do not lose. I play through "Sesame Street," "The Banana Splits" and "Diff'rent Strokes." I win two aces in a war and go on to accumulate most of the deck.

"Isn't this fun?" my daughter giggles.

I look across at her and grudgingly admit it is. Her happiness is contagious.

Shortly after 10:30, she wins. I surrender, bemoaning my fate, pretending to be devastated. "Poor Mommy," she comforts, climbing on my lap, winding her arms around my neck. "Don't be sad. I'll play with you later. You'll get a chance to win then."

She puts the cards in the kitchen drawer and walks upstairs to get ready for school. As I dress her, we talk about the children in her class.

"Who's your favorite friend?" I ask, assuming it is Rachael.

"You are," she tells me eagerly.

"But I'm just your mother," I say.

"You're my best friend, too," she insists.

"How come?"

"Because you play games with me and read me stories and because you're weird."

"Thanks a lot."

"Robbie says your weird. But I don't think you are. I love you."

"I love you, too," I say, hugging her.

After lunch, I fix Triscuits and peanut butter for her snack, zipper her winter coat and open the door to wait with her for the bus. It is 12:15 and I have done nothing.

"Here comes the bus," she yells, grabbing her lunch box in one hand and her Fisher Price tape recorder in the other.

She turns her face for a kiss goodbye and my heart winces a little because I know that in a few years I will miss her kisses and her games and her insistence that I am her best friend. I know that in a few years she will have a real best friend. She will not seek out my company. I will not be everything to her. She will not need me.

I watch her struggle up the steps of the school bus, burdened with her carry-ons, her coat bulky on her tiny frame, and my love for my smallest daughter, my close-to-the-ground person, burgeons.

I watch as the school bus closes its doors and shudders down the road. And I understand, with the wisdom that comes with age, why my father was never too busy to play with me. He knew all along what I am just discovering: that the house, the bills, the library, the responsibilities will all be there, still waiting for me, long after my daughter is grown and gone.

Is There a Tooth Fairy?

The question comes on the way to the movies, unprovoked, unexpected, unprepared for.

"I want you to tell me the truth, Mommy," my 10-year-old says. "Is there really a tooth fairy or are you the one who leaves the money?"

A few days before she had lost a tooth, wrapped it in foil and put it under her pillow. "Do you suppose the tooth fairy might leave more than a dollar this time?" she'd asked as I tucked her in. "Maybe a dollar and a quarter?"

"Tooth fairies don't carry change," I explained. "It'd weigh them down and then they couldn't fly. But I'll pay you two dollars if you give your tooth to me."

"You will?" she shouted, then furrowed her brow and looked at me suspiciously. "Why would you give me two dollars, Mom? What would you do with my tooth?"

"I'd plant it in the backyard with the daffodils Grandma gave me so that next spring I'd have another you."

"Oh Mommy," she said giggling, choosing an elusive but sane tooth fairy over her present but peculiar mother.

Two days later she popped the question.

"So tell me? Is she real or isn't she?"

"What do you think?" I say, my eyes on the road and not on her, afraid that questions about the tooth fairy will lead to other myth-shattering subjects.

* * *

"You have to tell me the truth. Is there really a Santa Claus?" I asked my own mother as we were walking through the parking lot on our way to 11:30 Mass. I had her cornered. If she lied she couldn't go to Communion. If she didn't go to Communion I'd know she lied. I looked at my mother. My mother looked at me. And with dozens of people milling around she burst into tears.

"Who told you?" she wanted to know. "Who ruined your childhood?"

I was in the sixth grade. I wore a bra bigger than she wore. I was in love with Mr. O'Neil, my sixth grade teacher, and was constantly singing "Teacher's Pet," and "Born Too Late." But my mother still thought I was a baby, and in a way I must have been, because I needed to hear the words from her. I needed her to tell me about Santa Claus.

* * *

"So what do you think?" I say to my own daughter. "Do you believe the tooth fairy is real? Do you want her to be real?"

"I think she's you," she says. "I sort of knew. I mean, really Mom, what kind of a person goes flying around in the middle of the night? What about Santa Claus? Is he real?

"What do you think?" I say, remembering my mother, and other conversations with my older son and daughter, understanding again, why they all ended in tears.

"Well, he knows who I am. Every year, he says 'Hi Julie. How are you?' But does he pay for the toys? Does he come down the chimney? Does he live at the North Pole?"

"If people can't afford to pay for the toys then he pays for them. He uses doors not chimneys. And he lives in a lot of different places, not just the North Pole."

There is silence in the car as she ponders this.

"What did you do with my teeth, Mommy?"

"I have them saved in a box at the top of the closet."

"Can I look at them later?"

"Sure you can. Any time you want."

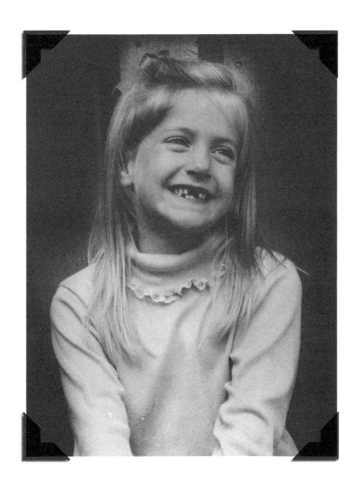

The Magic of a Carnival

I don't want to go. I'm tired. I have a sore throat and the night is damp and rainy.

But the children beg and my husband insists. So I pull on my warmest socks, grab some Vitamin C tablets for the road and tell myself to think happy thoughts. We are going to a carnival — in the middle of a monsoon.

"I can't wait to ride the Tilt-a-Whirl," shrieks a child from the back seat.

"That's for babies! I want to go on the rocket that tips upside down," shouts her brother.

"Why? So you can throw up like you did last year?"

I turn around, sharp words on my tongue, and notice my six-year-old smiling smugly as if she were remembering a sweet secret.

"And what do you want to do most?" I ask, my annoyance evaporating.

"I want Daddy to win me a bear just like Sarah's."

"Not many people win those bears," I tell her. "Sarah was lucky."

"Daddy will win one for me," she says, confident as a bumper sticker.

When we arrive the rain has stopped and the earth smells clean, like sheets flapping in a breeze. Excitement pulses in the air. I am suddenly glad I came.

In our town, the annual carnival is not thrown together on a slab of concrete. It is erected in a spacious field allowing the huge, glimmering mechanical creature with outstretched tentacles the space and freedom to breathe.

Dozens of rides beckon. A ferris wheel lights up the evening sky. A gyrating conclave of steel boxes whoosh in a circle. The Scrambler thunders, then creaks and moans.

Boys hug their girlfriends and husbands hug their wives.

Young and old push baby carriages while munching on popcorn or cotton candy or fried bread dough, all temporarily children.

My older two children hurry off with friends. "Let's go on a few rides before we play any games," I suggest to the youngest.

"Will you go on the ferris wheel, Daddy?"

They rush to the line, he striding and she skipping beside him. I watch as they soar, disappearing and appearing in a soothing, mechanical rhythm. Giggles spill down on me and I am warmed by the sound.

"What's next, Pumpkin?" he asks, scooping her from the ride into his arms. "Wanna see how handsome I can be?"

She giggles again as they race to the house of mirrors. The music of her laughter resonates, a counterpoint to the barker's howling and the hard rock that roars from the heart of the beast, grinding and groaning, spitting noise into the cool, spring night.

It comes, of course, as it must. The inevitable showdown. "Now, can you win me a bear like Sarah's?"

They approach the booth like soldiers entering a foreign land. Dozens of bears appear amused, their plastic eyes glistening, reflecting the lights that dance about them.

"Just put your money on a color," the barker cries. "If your color comes up you win yourself a bear. Fifty cents is all it takes. How about it, Mister?"

My daughter's eyes meet her father's and there is something close to awe in them. I wish we could leave right now.

"What color do you want, honey?" he asks.

"Yellow," she announces firmly.

People crowd together, placing their money on colors that

even Crayola hasn't identified.

"Why don't you toss the ball in?" the barker says to a boy about 12. "Whatever color she lands on is the winner."

Delighted with his sudden importance, the youngster scans the crowd and savors the moment. He holds the ball still, attracting all eyes, then hurls it into the small rectangle of colors. It thrashes against the bars, rolling from hole to hole. From red...to blue...to green...to yellow!

"I don't believe it. You won!" I scream.

"Sorry Ma'am. That's a lemon, not a yellow."

We try again. Another 50 cents is placed on yellow. A different crowd gathers, pushing its way to the game. But my daughter doesn't move. She hugs her spot like a catcher guarding home plate. Quarters clink into the tray. The bears' eyes grow brighter.

"Why don't you give it a shot?" the barker croons, handing the ball to my husband. He throws it too quickly, a grenade in his hands. It lands outside the rectangle and plunges to the ground.

"Out of practice, aren'tcha, Mister?" A grin doesn't hide his embarrassment. "Here, give it another try."

This time he is careful. The ball soars upward, then thumps as it falls into the rectangle and careens from color to color. It idles suddenly, resting in fuchsia, stalling in watermelon where it seems entrenched until, magically, miraculously, it sneaks into...yellow.

"I knew you'd win it for me, Daddy," my daughter says, hugging her bear with her arms and her father with her eyes.

"Looks like you're a hero, Mister," the barker roars, setting up for another game.

A little boy with a crewcut walking by pulls on the arm of a man in a Robert Young sweater. "Look, Grandpa. Can you win me a bear like hers?"

And as the older man reaches into his pocket and strides over to the booth, I can't help thinking that a special kind of magic is at work here. Because it is only at a carnival where, for a pocketful of change, anyone can take a chance and become a hero.

A House in the Country

The ducks triggered the memory. I was on the red line when I saw them — a proud ceramic mother leading her ceramic babies across a lawn no bigger than a mattress.

The lawn was emerald green, a patch of sod that seemed plucked from another place, the ducks bright and unblemished, not yet stained by soot from the train. They didn't belong where they were, squeezed in between cement and macadam. They didn't belong parading in the shadow of buildings and trains. They didn't belong in their surroundings any more than another set of ducks belonged camped out on our living room floor, ducks my mother saved for and bought at least a lifetime ago.

She had wanted them for months. Every week, after stopping at the butcher's and the grocer's, we'd head for Woolworth's where we would sit side-by-side at the long, formica counter. I would have a soda, and she would sip coffee and stare in the mirror facing us. From the beginning, you could see the ducks reflected in that mirror, the mother facing the wrong way, the babies following behind. My mother never stopped looking at them.

"Someday I'm going to buy those ducks," she declared the first time she saw them. "I'm going to buy them and put them right in the middle of the front lawn."

"But we don't have a front lawn," I reminded her.

"We will someday," she said. "We will when we get a house in the country."

"A house in the country." It was a phrase she uttered at least once a day, a group of words I always thought of as one. A "houseinthecountry" was my mother's constant dream.

She was a city girl, born, raised and married in brick and cement buildings. But there had been a time, a few years when she was a child, when her parents had rented a house with a garden and a huge front lawn. She yearned for those times. In the confines of the three-decker where she lived with my father and me, she would talk about what she remembered — rose bushes in the garden, flowers that grew wild by the side of the road.

She wanted that life again. She wanted a home, land, a garden, a front lawn.

She built a world around that dream. In the flat where we lived, across the hall from my bedroom, there was a room, a living room, my mother called it, though, in fact, no one lived there. The heat was turned off, the lights didn't work and the door was always closed.

In that room were all the items she bought for her dream, all the things she was saving for her "houseinthecountry."

Sometimes, when she was folding laundry or cooking dinner, I would push open the door to that room and gaze at the beige couch and the green velvet chair and the long mahogany coffee table that were destined for a living room someplace far away.

"But why can't we use them now?" I would ask. "We wouldn't wreck them."

"They're for our 'houseinthecountry,' " my mother would reply. And the conversation would end before it began.

The afternoon she purchased the ducks, I knew where they would go. I helped carry them home, the important package weighing me down but lifting me up somehow, making me feel as if I, too, were part of the dream. Like a child with a cherished toy, my mother unwrapped the ducks, set them in the center of the room, then sat and stared at them until the light faded from the window and the ducks became just shadows on the hardwood floor.

After that, it seemed the room belonged to them. When I

would look in, there they would be, caught in mid-step, strutting across the floor as if they, too, were in a hurry to get to the country.

Eventually they got there. Eventually they strutted all the way to the South Shore, nesting on a front lawn with a rose bush growing over a trellis and daffodils bordering the walk. They lived there for years until the rain wore away their eyes and a lawnmower ran over the smallest.

I had forgotten them, almost. I hadn't thought about them in years. But the train ride, that glimpse at someone else's dream, brought it all back: the special room, those afternoons in Woolworth's, all the hopes my mother had pinned to her "houseinthecountry."

The house is gone now; she sold it years ago. The country is gone, too, with its dirt roads and sprawling fields. Today her country is city with lower buildings.

But that's okay, because for a while it was everything she expected. For a while she was able to look out her window and see roses in bloom and ducks waddling across her lawn. For a while, her dream came true.

A Trying Phase

On a good day, I can see it's just a phase. That underneath the sighing, pleading, dirty-look giving, foot-stomping, thumping-up-the-steps person who just yesterday was a sweet little girl writing me notes that ended in "I love you," there really is this incredibly sensitive, likable, human being.

That's on a good day.

On a bad day it takes a leap of faith to believe in butterflies. "I only hope," my mother used to say, "that someday you have a daughter just like you."

Thanks Mom. You should be happy. Your wish is upstairs sulking.

Only a few hours ago she was downstairs smiling. That's the problem with 13. Thirteen is a chameleon, all sunshine and light. "Want me to set the table?" "Gee, I like your dress." "Mmm, this dessert is delicious!" Smiling, pleasant, accommodating, one moment; the next, sighing and sarcastic.

Of course, this time it was my fault. I should have known. I should have anticipated.

"So tell me the truth, Mom. Do you think I'm fat?" she asked, as I sat at the kitchen table reading the newspaper.

"No, I do not think you're fat," I said honestly.

"No, really. Tell me the truth. I promise I won't be mad at you. Do you think I'm fat?"

I looked across the table at pleading eyes.

"No, honey, I do not think you're fat."

"Well, maybe I should lose a few pounds anyway. What do you think?"

"If you think you'd feel better about yourself, maybe you should," I said. "It wouldn't be that hard to do."

What had I done? Yes, it was a reasonable suggestion, but not to 13. The words hung in the air like comic captions and I longed to grab them and stuff them back in my mouth.

"I knew it! You do think I'm fat!" she yelled, leaping from the chair, marching from the kitchen. Thump, thump, thump, thump, kaboom, kaboom, slam — seconds of silence followed by the mournful wails of Madonna, followed by the "Silent Treatment."

I'm getting used to it. Last week she didn't talk to me for 24 hours because of a bathing suit.

"So what do you think?" she asked standing before me in a sideless, backless thing that looked as if it should belong to her eight-year-old sister.

"I think you'd better be able to return it because if you can't, you wasted $30, because you are never leaving the house in that!"

So maybe I should have phrased it differently. So maybe I was a little too adamant in my criticism. Sigh, slam. Thump, thump, thump, thump, kaboom... followed by umpteen phone calls to friends complaining about the impossibility of existing in the same house as the Wicked Witch of the West.

I take solace in the knowledge that I am not alone in my suffering, that in fact, the world is full of 13-year-olds who were once smiley, loving little girls. I listen to friends relate stories and, if I were not experienced, I would think they exaggerated. But I know 13. I know that if children were born 13 and female, there would be no population problem. I know that 13 can be both moody and morose, sensitive and sensible in the same paragraph. I know 13 stands in front of a mirror for entire afternoons, painting and polishing and primping simply to make an entrance in the family room. I know 13 is up an hour before 11 or 12 to polish her nails and do her hair because how could you go to school without looking your best? I know 13 is never more than 10 feet away from a telephone, is consumed with boys (is there anything else?), has all the answers and is annoyingly selfish.

But sometimes, less frequently than I should, I see the other side of 13. I recognize the insecurity that makes it necessary to stand before the looking glass; the unease that comes when the phone is silent; the isolation of longing to be different, to be more than ordinary, yet needing to fit in. To be noticed, but not noticed. To remain a chameleon while envying the butterfly.

I look in a room where posters of Prince and Madonna cover the walls, where purple eye shadow and fake nails cover the bureau, while stuffed animals guard the bed. "When I grow up I'm going to live on a farm and have horses and a red Corvette and a pink telephone." Half woman, half child, not knowing which way to go.

"What do you think?" she asks me less frequently now. What do I think of purple hair and ears hidden by too many earrings and some boy saying she has nice hair. Do I think she has nice hair? Her perception of herself is only a reflection of what she sees in someone else's eyes.

I try to be careful with words. They have too many jagged edges; they hurt unintentionally.

I think you have beautiful hair, I tell her.

"Yeah, but you're my mother. You don't count," she says.

Anne counts. And Kim. And Kerri and Eileen and, of course, anyone male. That's the curse of 13.

"She'll get through it and so will you," my mother tells me. "It's just a phase."

I don't argue. I'm not 13. And for that, I'm enormously grateful.

More Than Just Kids

I t's not the National Guard, you know," my husband tells me as we drive through heat that shimmers. "He's not going to basic training. He's going to baseball camp. He'll have fun."

The brochure promises a good time. Professional ball players teaching youngsters who dream of hitting like Carl Yastremski and fielding like Dwight Evans. Daily baseball games, swimming, movies, lots of food. What more could a boy want?

I realize the camp will be a worthwhile experience for my son. I compute the facts: He is nearly 13; he has been away from home before, to the Cape with friends, to New Hampshire to visit an aunt.

Three children minus one equals less work, worry and woe. One less bell to answer, egg to fry, ad infinitum. I should be happy. But I'm not.

I'm not because my heart overrides reason. My son is only 12. He's never been away without someone who loves him close by. Will he be frightened? Lonely?

"This is not Beirut," his father quips. "He'll manage."

He'll manage, but will I?

"Are you going to cry, Mom?" comes the question from the back seat, concern marring the eagerness in the young voice.

I shake my head, not turning, not wanting to meet his eyes. I am not crying. But I am remembering.

* * *

3:30 a.m. Dublin, Ireland. February, 1969. A phone is ringing. It rings on and on. "Hello," a groggy voice mumbles across the wires, across the ocean.

My husband, in Ireland on business, had been sleeping, which was not unreasonable considering the time of the morning.

"I think I'm pregnant," I scream, as if by shouting I can shorten the miles that separate us.

The news could have waited. It wasn't confirmed, not even well established. But I was impatient, excited, anticipant, young. So I called.

Eight months later, when my son was born, I realized the meaning of my mother's liturgical diatribe, "wait-until-you're-a-mother-then-you'll-understand."

I understood. The miracle of life humbled me and filled me with pride. Had anyone seen a more beautiful child? Had there ever been such perfection?

I took pictures weekly for months documenting his rapid growth. I dressed him in miniature baseball shirts that hung to his ankles. I carted him to shopping malls simply to bask in the praise of strangers.

Like most new mothers, I was utterly obnoxious. My conversations were saturated with baby talk. "He rolled over today. Did you see him smile?" I bored anyone who would listen with talk of Pampers, Playtex nursers and bowel movements.

I learned the art of quiet consolation, a skill mastered by mothers everywhere who temper wails of hungry/angry/tired children while conducting phone conversations seemingly oblivious to the chaos about them. As he grew older and quieter I found myself caught between the pleasure of watching him grow and the pain of letting him go.

I think now, in retrospect, that in every relationship there is an intense period when the need to be with and talk about that other person usurps all other needs.

Eventually, that initial intensity mellows and a more subtle affection, a love that is less pervasive though no less dear, predominates.

I suppose it has to.

As my son grew, I let go, the tether taut at first, unraveling like the years, slowly, surely, ceaselessly. It is a part of life, this letting go. I know it. I understand it. Then why does it hurt so?

* * *

We reach the camp at noon. A bevy of boys in red baseball caps strut like roosters, reveling in their tentative independence.

We meet the counselors. They look earnest, dependable. I want to whisper, "Take care of him, my son." But I don't. I bite my lip and the impulse fades like breath on a mirror.

We go to his room. It is small. Neat. Nice. I make his bed and small talk while he unpacks.

Later, after registration, we prepare to leave. "Bye, Dad. Bye, Mom," he mumbles. For just a moment his confidence wavers like a candle flame caught in a sudden draft.

I touch him timidly, not wanting to embarrass him, yet needing to show my love.

He leaves us then, striding across the crowded gymnasium and in a moment he is just another red cap bobbing somewhere in the distance, indistinguishable from the crowd.

On the way home I find myself thinking of an incident that occurred earlier in the week.

A friend stopped by, a person who had never met my children. "Well, what do you think of them?" I asked after introductions had been made.

"They're all right," he replied. "They're just kids."

And that's what bothers me now. To strangers, to the world, they are all just kids. All the red caps. All the baseball pants and cleats. All the shaggy haircuts and mouths full of teeth. All the same.

But each is different. Special. Someone's child. Someone's son.

Summer

The Ghosts of Summers Past

Ghosts walk beside me today. A question has summoned them: "What did you used to do all summer when you were 11, Mom?"

The August air as thick as gauze has entrapped them, revenants from another time: Rosemary, Michelle, Ann Marie, Janet, all children I used to know; among them the child I used to be.

My daughter's voice is overshadowed by a chorus of high, thin voices sing-songing, "Red Rover, Red Rover send Ann Marie over." I feel Janet squeezing my hand, telling me not to let go as we steady ourselves for the impact. Stones crunch as Ann Marie gets ready. She's on her mark, gets set and GOES, crashing through our human barrier despite our solid stance. And for her effort, all she gets is to take one of us back to her team.

She does not pick me. She picks Janet and we play until the street lights come on, then race home, the silent click our signal to go in and wash up and take our places beside our parents in parlors cooled by a single fan to watch some variety show on a small black-and-white TV.

"It sounds pretty boring," my daughter says, switching channels on a big color TV. "I mean you didn't have cable or VCR's or swimming pools or anything."

The ghosts look at her and shake their heads. Janet says, "I don't remember being bored, do you? How come we weren't bored? What exactly did we do all summer?"

What did we do? We used to play, all day, every day, under sprinklers in our yards, at the beach if somebody's father were home to drive, or if it were too hot, in a cool cellar where we would read comic books and play cards and suck on fireballs and consume tall glasses of ice water until our stomachs hurt.

We used to go to the movies — two movies for a quarter

— every single Saturday, then walk to confession. We used to meet in the woods, behind the school for the deaf, have picnics there, sit in the shade and plan the rest of our lives. The woods were safe then, and the movies were, too — no ratings necessary for films like "The Spider" and "Heaven Knows Mr. Allison." And planning our lives seemed an adult thing to do.

I see myself in Mr. Tantillo's car, driving to a lake where I swim way, way out, then play horseshoes and sit in the shade in a forest of pines. I see scenes from "A Kiss Before Dying," from the back seat of my father's car where the mirror is always in the way. I smell popcorn, feel mosquitoes biting my legs, hear the Pledge of Allegiance at Girl Scout camp, taste hot toasted marshmallows and salt water taffy, and hear the music of the carousel at Nantasket. These are my memories of childhood summers. Are they real? Could all of this have happened? Was life ever so sweet?

"But didn't you go to gymnastics or play softball or do anything structured like that?" my daughter asks, unimpressed.

"Tell her how we used to do cartwheels and headstands on the front lawn," Rosemary says. "Tell her how people paid a whole nickel to see us stand on our heads at talent shows."

"I don't think that's going to impress her," I say.

"Didn't you ever go shopping? Or go out to eat?" today's child wants to know.

"Shopping? Ugh!" Michelle moans. "Who would want to go shopping? And who would want to eat out when you could eat for free at home."

"It was a different world," I try to explain to my daughter. "There weren't even any McDonald's around when I was your age."

"No McDonald's? Then there were only Burger Kings?"

I tell her there were neither, and she is stunned.

"So there were no McDonald's. No Burger Kings. No color TV. No movies to rent. No friends with swimming pools. No gymnastics and softball. Mothers didn't drive so they couldn't take you anywhere, and even if they could drive there wouldn't have been anyplace to go. I'm just glad I wasn't born when you were, Mom. Summers must have been totally dull."

My ghosts bristle at the word. They shout at my daughter that she is wrong. But she can't hear them and even if she could, she wouldn't understand. The childhood she knows is the childhood she loves. Only we who are older, who remember another time, long for one more ride on the carousel, one final summer when it would be possible simply to be.

Tuning Out Life

The woman arrives at the beach carrying a chaise lounge and a canvas bag, headphones hugging her ears, sunglasses masking her eyes, Nikes guarding her feet. She moves through the sand on tiptoe, as if it is unpleasant terrain.

She unfolds the chaise lounge, sits down quickly and takes off her shoes. She puts them in her bag, smears oil over her body, adjusts her Walkman and places a towel over her face. Then she leans back.

She is spending the day at the beach.

It is a golden day. The sun smiles a broad, even grin that spreads its glow across the sand, onto the rocks jutting to the sea, gilding houses clustered on a hill. A breeze hums, a soft familiar hymn.

My daughter and her friend drop their towels and race to the water eager to ride the waves, begging, "Hurry, Mommy. Hurry!" Their giggles crinkle like cellophane caught by the wind.

I walk to the water's edge and watch the waves quiver and crack, spilling children back onto the shore. Diamonds of salt and sand shimmer on their skin. Pieces of sky flash in their eyes. A foghorn bleats, a plane growls, and the children look up to see a banner flapping: "From the Director of Gremlins — The Explorers."

They tire in time and return to the blanket. Across the street, men are working. A lawnmower purrs while hammers, molding new shingles to old wood, clap their approval.

On the chaise lounge, the woman remains. She doesn't move. She doesn't flinch. The waves chant, the children laugh, the men at work call to one another. But she is impervious to it all, a song on the radio more important than life being played out around her.

The children beg for lunch, though it is still morning. They unwrap sandwiches, open the box of Cheez-its and poke straws through their already warm box drinks. A lone seagull squawks above our blanket, cackles almost, demanding attention. Perhaps it is lonely. Perhaps it is calling for friends. Within seconds, dozens appear. They land in front of us. My daughter and her friend are awed.

"Can't we give them some peanut butter and jelly, Mommy? Do you think they'd like it?"

At first, the gulls do not move. The wind ruffles their feathers; strays swoop down to join the crowd, but the birds remain still, etched in black and white. Dozens of steely eyes study us. Seconds stretch, fragile seconds, until, at some invisible signal, the birds in unison begin to peck, devouring soft white bread that oozes jelly and peanut butter and sand.

When the bread is gone, the gulls retreat. They flap their wings and scream their high-pitched goodbyes. They sound like windows being rubbed and squeaked dry.

I look at the woman on the chaise lounge. She has not moved. She has not seen. She has not heard. Her skin shines with oil and sweat. The towel on her face seesaws with every breath. I think she is sleeping.

The children and I search for sea glass, more jewels than broken bottles, soothed by the tide. Sea glass is rare these days because of plastic containers; therefore we treasure it more.

We walk along the sand that is furrowed, as if deep in thought, and the children play tag with the tide.

"What's this?" my daughter asks, bending to pick up something that looks like alligator skin.

I don't know, I say. A man, walking behind us, overhears and stops to explain.

"Where are you from?" he asks, not expecting me to say

from here.

"You're from here and you don't know what this is?" He shakes his head, then explains that this skin-like thing is nothing but sand molded by snails. "It's called a sea collar," he tells us.

Sea collars are everywhere. How have I never noticed them? We collect them along with sea glass. In the distance sailboats hug the edge of the world. When they disappear it looks as if they have really fallen off.

We return to the blanket, our arms full of treasures. The sky has turned a pale shade of blue, a silent ocean, its waves inching along.

While we were gone, the woman moved. She rolled over. All afternoon she keeps her back to the sun.

She leaves before we do, as briskly as she arrived. She sits up, takes her shoes from the bag, puts them on, folds her chaise lounge and hurries across the sand.

She never walked to the water. She never walked in the sand. She was here, but wasn't.

She doesn't realize how much she missed.

Hazel

It was a perfect summer day. Wildflowers nodded from the sides of the road and danced in the fields usually strewn with Budweiser cans. Young people rode bikes and old people pruned gardens. The entire world seemed to be outdoors doing something. On this perfect day, I visited Carney Hospital.

For a hospital, Carney isn't bad. It's modern and it's clean. But it isn't the Ritz. And it isn't home.

The contrast between the hospital environment and the "outside" world has struck me dozens of times. But on this day, the closed windows, antiseptic smells and patient lethargy seemed more pronounced. Maybe because on Dorchester Avenue I'd noticed a lady in a flowered housecoat watering geraniums on her front porch. Maybe because I'd watched a gray-haired man with a limp pushing a child on a tricycle. Or maybe just because the car windows had been opened and the sounds of summer — lawnmowers whining, bicycles clacking, planes roaring, car radios blaring and birds chattering — made me achingly aware there is more to life than wheelchairs and hospital beds.

I walked down the hall of the third floor, and the day's beauty dimmed, becoming as indistinct as the memory of someone who died years before. The flawless sky and the robust trees receded and were replaced by shiny linoleum and colorless walls.

I noticed Hazel immediately. She was there, among a group of old people lining the hall like weary defenders of a lost cause. They sat slouched in wooden chairs, white-haired ladies in white johnnies bent like trees in winter, their burdens, like snow, too heavy for their frail limbs. The looks in their faces — of fear, resignation and regret — were the result of more than physical suffering. Their long lives had turned into long deaths.

Hazel stood out among them, not just because she wore over her johnny a cable-knit sweater the color of bachelor's buttons, but because Hazel lends dignity to a crowd. She is frail and forgetful — but wonderful.

I pulled up a chair beside her. She has few visitors because she has committed the grievous offense of outliving most of her family and all of her friends. I met her because she shared a room with my mother. And for some reason, a reason I don't understand, I fell in love with her.

I don't know much about Hazel other than that she was born in another century and has endured more years and seen more changes than I can imagine. She was married twice, had two sons and buried one of them.

Her first husband was an entertainer and she sometimes performed with him. "I was just a bit of window dressing," she said in a moment when the past was suddenly clear.

But Hazel has memory problems, a result of old age and a hard life. Hallucinations march through her mind, stand guard in the corner of her consciousness and direct her thoughts. Her frailty and confusion confine her to the hospital. But she is restless, constantly walking around, asking for her son, aching to go home, clutching her pocketbook, which holds all her earthly possessions — a couple of letters, two pair of glasses and a comb.

The first time I met Hazel she asked me to phone her mother. "My mother will murder me for being up here," she explained, her eyes bright blue marbles. "I have to go home right now or I'll get killed."

"I'll call your mother and explain that you're safe," I told her holding her hand, a hand as fragile as a corsage she might have pressed years before after a high school dance.

"Do you think she'll understand?" she asked, trembling.

"I'm sure she will."

So I phoned a woman dead for 50 years and Hazel's face softened and her eyes flashed when I told her her mother wasn't angry.

Hazel might be confused about where she is but she knows who she is. Her memory is a kaleidoscope of past and present, constantly mixed up and impossible to maintain. 1908 sits right next to today, but it doesn't matter somehow because it's her spunk and her tenacity that put fire in her eyes. Being with Hazel is like having tea on the "Queen Mary." At 87, despite a lack of God-given teeth, fine clothing and a proper sitting room, she is a lady.

"There's no sense fretting about being old," she tells me all the time. "It happens to all of us. When I was young, I remember my mother rushing to visit this one or that one in the hospital. 'It gets lonely in there,' she said. So when I got older I remembered her words and did my share of visiting. But now there's no one left."

She shrugs and smiles and squeezes my hand. She's not complaining. Hazel is a lady. And a lady never complains.

Maine Draws Her Back

The muffin lady isn't here this year. She has decided to remain in St. Petersburg where she spends the winters and where there are happy hours every day. She will return, however. In her 70s, her body might be reluctant to suffer the Northeast chill that can seep through old bones even on summer days; flesh and blood might yearn to stay where it is. But her soul will pull her back. Florida is not Maine, after all. Florida, for all its sun and heat is static, and cannot compete with the spirited coast.

The muffin lady is the only regular who has not returned to our favorite inn; a college boy takes her place, walking around the dining room offering muffins and rolls to guests. But Brenda is there by the door as usual to seat everyone and Peggy is still behind the front desk and Eva comes out of the office regularly to give old friends a hug. And there are, of course, all the Dugases saying hello and shaking hands.

"Is this what you love about Black Point Inn?" friends ask when I tell them I am counting the days until it is time to go there again.

In February, when the confirmation arrives, I tape it on the refrigerator door and begin the long wait. Twelve more weeks, 10 more weeks. Am I impatient to talk to old friends again? Is it they who draw me back?

Of course they do. Yet the lure is more than people. For even the first time we came, two adults and three children, strangers to this place, I knew instantly that I had finally arrived at the exact place where I wanted to be.

Physically handsome, the inn has the "same time next year" intimacy, with its mahogany furniture and hardwood floors, its fresh flowers and afternoon tea, the ocean or the promise of it beckoning from every window, the strong, heady smells of burning wood and briny sea.

Yet it isn't just the physical things, as it isn't just the people who keep pulling me back. It is something more, some combination of things.

Is it that everything is the same here, but everything is different? Seeing the same people, walking along the same beach, climbing the same rocks, bike riding along the same roads — these all satisfy a need for the familiar, the comfortable; a need to go home again. But all these things satisfy an opposing need for change, too, because the familiar is in constant flux: the beach, the cliff walk, the color of the water, the hue of the sky, fading, brooding, sparkling, dimming, brightening.

I walked along the rocks this morning and mist like a bride's veil covered the houses on the distant shore. Now, a few hours later, the houses are as clear and defined as cutouts pasted on a backdrop of sky and sand by some fastidious child.

This morning, waves ate up boulders and spat them back as if they were watermelon seeds. Now the sea is spent, gently rocking back and forth.

Is it this view then that makes Prout's Neck my favorite place in the world? No, for there are, I know, more spectacular places. I've seen them, through a bus window, on a train, from a helicopter: Kauai, the Grand Canyon, the Rocky Mountains, Denali National Park — lusher, bigger, grander places.

And yet I love it here best.

I sit on a rock and watch the ocean. The surf pounds, ducks float by, gulls swoon, a cold breeze carries the taste of salt, and I am overwhelmed by a moment so right, so perfect, that I wonder at the audacity of ever daring to hope for more.

Slow down, the moment reminds me. Stay a while. Think.

Feel. Dream. Imagine. Remember lying on a blanket and watching the clouds, trying to count the stars at night, looking for a four-leaf clover, searching for a rainbow's end.

I did all these things once, when days had their own rhythm and time seemed as endless as the sea; I did these things when I was a girl and could stand in June and see clear through a succession of carefree days all the way to September.

Here I am this girl again, sitting on a rock, seeing clear through today all the way back to then and all the way ahead to eternity.

And so it is this that ultimately lures me here: Time — to reflect, to dream. Unhurried time in an unhurried place that feels like home used to feel when I was a pampered child.

Passing Friendships

At another time, we wouldn't have met. We might have passed on the street, nodding maybe; or we might have made eye contact at Wendy's or Burger King. But we would not have spoken. We would have studied signs and prices, hugging our privacy as protectively as we hug our children.

But a conference brought us together. A shared interest led us to a room where dozens of strangers exchanged hellos. And we talked. I don't remember who spoke first or what was said. Only that afterward, there was Teresa, beckoning, smiling, saving a place for me, talking about a dirt road that cut clear across the mountain, sharing local history and some personal history, dropping pieces of her life like bread crumbs I might want to follow.

We made an unlikely pair, me with my broad r's and suburban ways; her with a twang you could sing to and a tongue quick with folklore. Thirteen years, 2,000 miles and a lifestyle should have separated us.

Yet we were together.

The first night, after a meeting that lasted long after sunset, we walked outside to rain that glazed the narrow road, to thunder that threatened to rip the earth apart. I ran to my rented car with an assurance I didn't feel, yelling "Good night Teresa. See you tomorrow!" The world was so black that mountain fused with sky. The storm wailed and I shivered. I started the car and turned on the radio but there was only static. I would have sold my soul right then for traffic and lights and people. I wanted to desert the car and chase Teresa across the lot and yell, "Hey, wait for me!" But I couldn't see where she'd gone and she wouldn't have heard me anyway.

Yet somehow she must have heard because at the end of the lot she was waiting, her orange Rabbit a welcome shadow that crawled down the mountain in second gear, lighting the way, breaking trail, leading me to the bottom, to the highway, to civilization.

"Thank you," I said the next morning when we met at breakfast. We were still strangers and yet we weren't. She smiled, a huge grin that involved her whole face. "I had a feeling you might need some help," she said.

After that, we had lunch together every day. "God made a thousand shades of green and not one of them clash," she said as we sped down the mountain. On those rides Teresa talked. She talked about how clouds trapped in the valley create sudden rainstorms; how in the spring deer wander onto the road. How Sopris is her favorite mountain, because in the early evening, after work, it welcomes her home. She told me that Teddy Roosevelt came to Glenwood Springs to hunt and that the Teddy Bear is named after him. And she talked about herself and her history in the same matter-of fact-tones.

She talked about a father who beat her and a stepfather who tried to rape her and how she left home at 13, afraid he'd succeed.

She talked about dropping out of school and turning to drugs and all the wrong people and living a fast life and keeping a diary and reading it now, and remembering.

She talked about her husband, how they met, how she thought he was cute but boring. How he changed her life.

"Kirk took me to his church and it's like they all adopted me," she said. "These people were strangers but they cared. There was this lady named Tilly and when she heard that me and Kirk were getting married she said, 'Teresa, I'd be honored if you let me make your wedding gown.' Honored! Another lady offered to make our wedding cake, and I said sure cuz' I didn't want to hurt her feelings. Then when I saw the cake I couldn't believe it. It was pink with white lacy frosting all over it; it must have taken her a week to make."

Teresa showed me pictures of her wedding. I was disappointed. They were just pictures. They couldn't capture the energy of the girl beside me, a girl who belonged to the mountains, a large girl with huge eyes that took in worlds, a girl with hands that were constantly gesturing, a girl God had made big to accommodate an extra-large heart.

On the way to the airport, when the conference was over, I was confined with dozens of other cars in Glenwood Canyon. Teresa had warned me. "They're puttin' in an interstate so give yourself an extra hour," she'd said.

I shut off my car and looked around at rock and earth and sky and wondered if Revlon came here every morning, to bronze and polish and highlight. And I thought, if Teresa were here she would know the names of these rocks, and she would know what kinds of flowers were growing at the side of the road. She would tell me why a tree perched on what looked like slate continued to thrive, and why clouds don't get trapped between these canyon walls.

At another time, in another place, our differences would have kept Teresa and me apart. We would have remained strangers. We would have sought out someone like ourselves, someone who reflected our values.

And that would have been a pity. I would have missed so much.

To Be Young Again

George Burns may wish he were 18 again, but if I could go back in time, I'd become eight or nine or 10.

I miss everything about being a little kid. I miss "I Remember Mama" and Little Lulu comic books and having a pocketful of mint juleps, two for a penny, and maybe a few squirrels that you could chew all day because your teeth weren't full of fillings back then.

I miss the way my clothes used to look in my old maple dresser, crisp and creased and orderly, shirts in one drawer, shorts in another, visible proof of my mother's love.

I miss walking downstairs in the morning, seeing my mother in the kitchen, hearing her voice ("Cereal or eggs?") watching her pack my lunch, ("Bologna or peanut butter?") kissing her every day, the very last thing before leaving for school.

I miss having my biggest worry be whether Rosemary would beat me on that day's test (she almost always did) and whether, if I begged, she'd give me some of her potato chips. (They were "Wise" and she almost always did this, too.)

I miss recess and jumping rope and playing "Anybody in my way gets a five cent boot" and doing cartwheels and pretending to find four-leaf clovers and riding my bike "no hands" and singing "R-A-T-T-L-E, S-N-A-K-E spells rattlesnake" and "Red Rover, Red Rover, send Ann Marie over" and counting the days until summer vacation.

I miss summer vacation most of all. Dozens of days. Thousands of hours. All that time. All that freedom *with nobody telling you what to do.*

It meant freedom to read Betty Cayanna books all night long; freedom to sleep over at Rosemary's any day of the week; freedom to wander for hours in the woods, to play in streams and sit with Rose under a tree and plan our entire lives. Freedom to play jacks and marbles and stay outside, until the streetlights came on. Freedom to run, to think, to dream; to go to the beach or hide out in the cellar; to be with friends or to be alone. Everything, every option, was possible.

This isn't exaggerated reverie. I'm not inventing the past. This is the way it was. And I miss it, every moment. Not always, of course. Being an adult has a few advantages. You get to drive a car (though unfortunately you have to pay for it, too); plus you get to eat anything you want, and not eat anything you *don't* want, which, when I was a kid, seemed like an incredibly exciting reason to hurry and grow up.

Now, despite the fact that no one forces me to eat peas anymore, when May slips into June and the countdown begins — when it's three weeks, then two weeks, then no weeks until summer vacation — I wander around unhappily stuck in this adult body in search of the magic door through which I can walk and become a child again.

For a time I actually found that door. For all the years my children were young, their summer vacations were mine, too. Mine weren't as unburdened as theirs. I couldn't go to the playground with them and make gimp bracelets. But I could play with their gimp when they came home. I couldn't wander off to the beach whenever the mood struck. But I could wander off more than I can now. Their freedom was mine and I reveled in it. I made lists of books to read and threw away lists of chores. I played more than I worked, and life slowed down as it always had. Maybe I didn't do cartwheels on the front lawn, but I jumped rope out back, and if I had lost the ability to ride "no hands," at least I was still pumping away trying to keep up with them.

But now, suddenly, surprisingly, life has outdistanced me. Two of my children are grown up. Now their summer vacations are full of jobs and social obligations. I guess I have grown up, too, because my calendar is crowded with appointments and deadlines and meetings. In the maze of schedules, between their obligations and mine, there is no down time, no stretch of days with nothing to do, no spontaneous rides to the beach, no picnics, no old-fashioned two-month, laid-back, lazy, lingering summer vacation.

This isn't a tragedy, I know. This is life in the grown-up world. Grown-ups don't get to spend July and August on a chaise lounge reading whatever they want. Grown-ups don't get to goof-off just because it's a beautiful day. In the grown-up world, July isn't much different from January. Life and work must go on.

Which is why from my office window I gaze out on summer mornings and ache to be young again.

One Perfect Day

The traffic is miserable. Cars grind to a stop in Dorchester then stammer along for miles. Tractor-trailers and trucks are everywhere — ahead of me, behind me, next to me. I can't see or hear or smell anything but truck.

"Maybe we should go home. Maybe this isn't such a great idea," I say to the two nine-year-olds in my back seat. "It's going to take a long, long time to get to Canobie Lake. Maybe we should try another day."

"I don't mind if it takes a long time," my daughter's friend says. "I love trucks. I love looking at them up close."

That makes one of us, I think. But I look in the rear-view mirror and see two eager, smiling faces and know I can't turn around, no matter how much I want to.

So we forge ahead, over hill, over dale, until eventually we arrive. The children bolt from the car, eager, enthusiastic, but I lag behind, already tired and dreading the ride home.

I haven't been to Canobie Lake in years. When I was small, I was taken by my father, who never had to be coerced into going to an amusement park. "Come on, Dot," he'd say to my mother. "Come with us." But she'd decline, claiming she had work to do or clothes to iron. "You two go and have a good time."

We always did. I suppose in memory the good times have become better times. I suppose I've mixed up all those early years, combined them so the dozen afternoons and evenings we spent riding the Ferris wheel, playing the Wheel of Fortune, selecting the duck with the magic number have been transformed into one perfect day.

I don't expect that perfect day now. I enter Canobie Lake Park knowing it won't be the same. The rides won't be as wild, the lights won't burn as bright, the music won't be as magical.

And yet...

I hear it immediately, the sound like a marching band, light and brisk and merry, full of energy and promise. The calliope sings out like Ethel Merman, beckoning in cheerful, hopeful notes. "Hurry! Hurry! Hurry!" it seems to cry. "Come here for a good time."

The children rush, and so do I, under a sky so flawlessly blue, on a day so ideally warm that stepping into a long shadow is like walking in front of an open refrigerator door.

I sit on a bench and forget about the traffic, forget about the ride home, forget — for a while — that I am an adult. The music has snared me, the bright lights, the shining, grinning horses. I sit back and relax.

It's then I notice the man. He stands out in the crowd of babies, toddlers and children, a well-scrubbed old man with white hair and a red Canobie Lake shirt sitting John Wayne-tall on the shiniest, biggest horse of all. Or perhaps it just seems shiniest and biggest because of him. I don't know. I don't understand. But I watch him as the music plays, as the carousel spins. I watch him get lost in the sound, his hands moving to the beat as if he is a conductor, his lips humming along. He is old but only in age. His skin is illuminated as if a candle burns inside and, even in repose, his face wears a smile.

When the ride stops, I watch him help the children off. I can't hear what he says, but I see the looks they give him, gazes they usually save for Santa Claus. When the carousel is empty, when the last child is gone, he walks toward the exit, and I half expect him to disappear.

But he doesn't. He delays the next ride for a group of screaming teenagers. "Hurry," he shouts, gesturing, smiling. Then he checks the strap of every small child before he steps down from the carousel, before the ride begins again.

Donald Baumgartner is 70. His wife died six months ago. "I joined a senior citizen club, and that was okay, but this is better. Working here is wonderful. These kids are fighters. A few weeks ago they brought in a group of handicapped children. One boy was paralyzed from the waist down. It took three of us to get him on a horse.

"But then there he was, sitting straight as an arrow, and I went up to him and said, 'You just close your eyes now, son, and imagine you're riding a real horse, riding over mountains, over plains, all on your own.' And the music started and that boy closed his eyes, and you should have seen him. You should have seen the look of rapture on his face.

"My wife and I, we were married for 33 years, but we never had any children, you see."

He says, "my wife," and his eyes brim with tears, and the light inside him dims a little. In that moment, in that second, he is ordinary again, just an old man in too much pain.

But as we speak, a child approaches, and then another, and before long there is a line of them, pointing, smiling. And the light inside Mr. Baumgartner returns, Tinkerbell saved by the clapping of hands.

My daughter and her friend leave the carousel for other rides. But all afternoon, I return to look at Mr. Baumgartner. He doesn't wear down. He doesn't get mean as the hour grows late. All day he smiles and checks safety straps and waits for running children, energized, thrilled, brightened by it all.

One perfect day. That's what he's making for every child who steps onto his ride. One perfect day. That's what they're giving back to him. In succession. A reason to get up in the morning. A reason to live.

Time to Smell the Roses

This is what people say: Things are too crazy these days. Life is too hectic. I have too much to do and so little time.

It's the truth, isn't it? Summer is supposed to be the slow-down-and-smell-the-roses season. But who has the time? The roses bud and the roses bloom and we hurry past thinking that tomorrow we'll take time to revel in their fragrance, to cut a few and arrange them in a vase and set them in the middle of a room, in the middle of a table, and maybe even invite a few friends over.

But tomorrow comes and it isn't any different from today; tomorrow goes, and roses and friendships die on the vine.

Last weekend I worked both mornings in my front yard. I cut the grass and edged the walk and weeded the flower beds, then drove to the nursery and bought annuals to plant. I was doing exactly what I wanted to do. But as I was digging neat holes for the already blooming marigolds and dusty miller, it occurred to me that I had never once seen my mother planting flats of pre-grown flowers. She planted seeds: bachelor buttons begun inside in the early spring for a space by the back door, daisies and zinnia nurtured for a rock garden in the back yard. Seeds, a packet of 100, cost what back then? A dime? A quarter?

The flowers I was planting cost a lot more. But they were convenient — already grown, easier to tend, and they immediately brightened the yard.

Immediate. Convenient. Easy. These are the key words. I wanted the flowers when I wanted them. That they cost far more than the seeds didn't matter.

I never got around to working in the back yard last weekend. There the gardens are still overrun by weeds, the shrubs remain overgrown and the grass is almost two feet high.

The gardens. This is another key word. My mother had a rock garden and a tiny plot by the back door, a manageable amount of nature to try to tame. I have *gardens* and cannot keep up with the trimming, the weeding and the pruning. My yard and its gardens, small compared to my neighbors', crystalizing the essential difference between life in my parents' day and life now.

My parents' yard was small. Their house was small. They shared one car. They drove on roads, not highways. They had one television, one telephone, one record player. They didn't eat out a lot. They didn't take long weekends or go on yearly vacations. No one vacationed, as in flew to Disneyland or the Bahamas for a week. Even the youngest couple in my neighborhood had only been as far as Niagara Falls.

Big, magnificent, expensive, wonderful THINGS didn't exist back then, at least not for ordinary working people; the world didn't flaunt a host of easily financed toys. I can't think of a single person with whom I grew up who had a two car garage, a living room AND a family room, multiple bathrooms, a car for everyone in the family, a lawn that was installed in one afternoon, a backyard swimming pool, a gas grill, a dishwasher, or even a clothes dryer.

If we had settled for what our parents had we'd be in better shape today. But we wanted bigger and better; Bigger houses, better yards, our own cars, highways that could get us places faster, big color TVs connected to cable so we can get dozens of stations, VCRs, sound systems, not just record players and not just in our homes but in our cars, as well. Video cameras, compact disks, contact lenses, family vacations, and on and on it goes.

And, oh, how I love all these things. But everything has a

price. Nothing is free. And so we have more than our parents had, but we also have less. It's a Faustian trade off. We pay for our toys, our luxuries and our conveniences with time; time spent earning the money to buy them, time spent enjoying them, and time spent caring for and fixing them.

If I had a smaller yard, I would have more time to smell the roses. But the back yard demands my attention — the grass is getting higher, the woods are growing stronger — and in my haste to tend to these, I hurry past the roses in bloom and catch only a breath of their sweet bouquet.

The Snapshot

My cousin Terry sent the picture. Terry from California, who flew into Boston this summer and visited my mother one sunny afternoon.

The picture is of the two of them. Terry, a pretty girl with light brown hair and big Irish eyes, hugging my mother, who is smiling right into the camera. My mother is sitting in a wheelchair out on the porch where on good days she loved to sit, smoking her Benson & Hedges, feeding the birds, watching the world go by.

My aunt must have taken the picture. She was the one who drove Terry to the nursing home. She was the one who later told me they'd visited. But I forgot, because Terry was here just one day and the summer passed and my mother died, and when the picture arrived a few weeks ago with a note that said, "I thought you'd like to have this," I held it in my hand and stared at it as if it contained the secret to eternal life.

Maybe it does.

My mother looks happy in the picture. She is sitting up straight, her chin high, the sun gentle behind her, bathing her in soft, tender light. Maybe she was happy because my aunt was behind the camera, making a wisecrack, making her laugh.

My aunt could always make my mother laugh. Even on the worst days, when there was no sun and she couldn't sit up or go outside, and the pain in her body was unbearable, if you mentioned that Lorraine was coming, my mother would cheer up. "My baby sister," my mother always called her. "My baby sister is coming today."

Maybe my mother was happy that day, too, because the sun was bright and the day warm and the pain in her body only danced instead of screeched, allowing her to enjoy the heat on her arms and the birds at her feet and the guy across the street who waved to her and the sound of traffic and the whistle of the train and her baby sister and her brother's daughter who'd come all the way from California to see her.

The shutter clicked and the moment passed. I know this. I know the day ended, and my aunt drove home and Terry went back to California and the birds flew away and the pain returned. The picture is only of a single moment.

And yet I have it here beside me, proof that there was this moment and other ones, too, not caught on camera. Eternal life, in a way. For I had been remembering not my mother's smile, but my mother's pain. I had been recalling hospital stays and setbacks, disappointments and frustrations, not the small moments of joy that kept her going and made her smile.

"How can you stand it out here?" I used to ask when I would find her on the shadeless porch in the heat of day. The sun was too hot and the traffic too loud and the train when it passed made talking impossible. Didn't the noise bother her?

"I like the sounds of people going places," she'd say, a longing in her eyes. "I like watching the birds fly and the train carry people away. It makes me remember running for a train in high heels. It makes me think about all the places I've been."

The picture makes me think not just of this moment but of all the others when, if a photograph had been taken, it would have caught my mother smiling.

A Glimpse of Beauty

It doesn't happen often. The last time was a year ago in the Canadian Northwest when what began as a solitary walk on a morning wrapped in mist ended in something else, something close to a glimpse of God.

While everyone slept, I wandered along the edge of Lake Louise, a lake fed by glaciers, whose water is more turquoise than blue, aqua too thin a word to describe its color. Behind the lake, enfolding, almost protecting it, were huge, jagged mountains cloaked in patches of fog thick as angel hair, that crept down toward the water and hovered there.

At first glance, it seemed as if the lake were boiling, as if the fog were steam from an enormous cauldron. But that was only if you looked quickly. I sat on a patch of wet grass and watched the lake and studied the mountain, and the feeling came. Not all at once, like a revelation, but slowly, steadily, the way the fog kept rolling to the water.

A chorus line of tall, leggy pines bordered the lake on both sides and formed a pair of wide parentheses that led the eye to a spot directly across from where I sat. There the mountains converged, glazed by a glacier frozen in motion. From thousands of feet away I could feel the energy in that freeze-framed cloak of ice, stopped in an instant by something infinitely bigger and more powerful than what I was seeing. My breath was frosty and it was cold where I sat shivering, but I was warmed and somehow comforted by what I felt around me.

Moments passed and clouds marched by, almost in procession, as if to pay homage to something I couldn't see but was beginning to sense. The fog rose and fell, appeared and disappeared in silent rhythm. Then without applause, without introduction, an invisible curtain lifted, the fog parted and the sun emerged, strong and bright and warm. For seconds, it seemed the earth held its breath. Nothing moved. Not the fog, not a bird, not even a fly. The lake was perfectly still, no ripple disturbed its sheen, and it seemed to be not a lake at all but a huge mirror reflecting the eye of God. It was a moment of unutterable beauty, a moment without future or past, an instant complete in itself.

The moment passed. The sun bowed and the curtain closed, and the mountains were again shrouded in white. It began to rain, and the rain broke the mirror and the mountain shattered into slivers of light and the slivers danced on the water's surface.

I should have been cold, the sun hidden; and unhappy, the moment passed. But I had been touched by something and that something lingered. I felt grateful for being a part of a feeling I didn't quite understand, a feeling that both exalted and humbled me.

I've felt this way before, in other places, at other times. In the dark of an auditorium watching a dance recital, a hundred little girls all smiles and curls, literally putting their best feet forward. How could I not be awed and elevated and thankful for the privilege of simply watching? For the gift of being an insignificant part of it all?

I've felt this way staring into nursery windows where lives lie wrapped in pink and blue. And I've felt this way when I've looked at my own children, really looked at them. Where did they come from? How was I so blessed? Even now, after years of motherhood, their being overwhelms me. Why them? Why me? Who made it this way?

It isn't always like this, of course. No daily epiphanies. Most times I see what I expect. Flaws. Weeds. But then in the notes of a song, in the eyes of a child, in the presence of a friend, on the shores of a beach, in the silence of a mountain,

I am somehow elevated and made to remember to give thanks.

This glimpse of something better, whether an intimation of heaven or simply a reminder that what we have here isn't all thorns, is what makes life worthwhile.

Building on Shifting Sand

T he first day they sculpted a dragon. All morning they worked, carrying pails full of dry sand to the stretch of beach where the water lapped lethargically, making its slow, inevitable retreat.

Painstakingly they molded the creature. She formed its long, serrated tail. He shaped its sturdy body. Together they searched for sea grass bronzed by the sun for its fiery tongue, then scoured the shore for black, oval rocks which, when placed on both sides of the creature's head, would make him not only sinister, but real. When they finished, they stood and joined the crowd, which had gathered to admire their work.

"But what's it attacking?" a freckled boy cried out. "Dragons don't go after people on the beach. They need knights and castles."

Perhaps to accommodate the boy or maybe just to please themselves, the couple began to construct a castle. They fashioned intricate turrets and spindly spires using wet sand sifted slowly through their fingers. They worked meticulously and relentlessly as the swollen summer sun glared from its sovereign position and the sea silently changed direction and began its greedy return to the shore.

By early afternoon, everyone on the beach was talking about the magnificent castle and the dragon which looked so real. Women put down their novels and children stopped splashing each other to hurry down the beach and gaze at the incredible sand creature and castle.

The pair turned up again the next afternoon. This time they created a mammoth mouse poised on outstretched paws just inches from a triangular hunk of cheese. Again, a crowd gathered and their delight and praise rose above the pounding surf, sounding like a prayer chanted in unison in a church full of believers.

Yet even as they stood together marveling at the creature, the tide was approaching. Waves licked the shore and stretched their eager tongues to reclaim what was theirs only hours before.

"Is this mouse going to be wrecked like the dragon was, Daddy?" a small girl asked in a voice trembling with tears.

"I'm afraid so," her father replied. "If you want, we can walk back to the blanket and you won't have to watch."

"No, I'll stay," the child said.

The crowd grew silent as the tide approached, then gasped as a wave swooped and swallowed the giant cheese in a single gulp. Succeeding waves gnawed at the mouse, taking tiny, teasing bites. First a paw. Then an ear. Next an eye, eroding the creature until it was just an indistinguishable hulk of sand.

"But why did they bother? Why did they waste all of their time making it if they knew it was just going to get wrecked?" the little girl asked her father.

"Because they enjoyed making it," the man replied. "And, I suppose, because they know that what they do makes people happy."

The little girl looked at him quizzically.

"The dragon made you happy, didn't it?"

"I suppose," she said.

"And you were sad yesterday when there was no dragon, right?"

"Right."

"And today you were all excited when you saw the mouse, weren't you?"

The child nodded.

"Well then, cheer up. Think what you would have missed if there had never been a dragon or a mouse. Nothing lasts forever, you know," he said, draping his arm around his daughter's shoulders and hugging her to him.

Nothing lasts forever. Not you and not me. Not our heroes or our fantasies. Not even our dreams. We build our castles and sea monsters, our reputations and lives, our families and careers all on shifting sand. And the geological fact is that, inevitably, the tide will come in and destroy what we've spent a lifetime creating.

So why do we work, strive, achieve, struggle to accomplish something if, in the end, our achievements, our possessions, the accumulations of a lifetime are destroyed?

Ideally we strive because we love what we do. But if we're lucky, our accomplishments will be remembered — if only by one small child.

Fall

Sadness of September

They are quarreling over a basketball. A minute ago it was forgotten, hidden among the weeds. Now one post-pubescent is yelling, "I had it first!" while the other screams, "Yeah, but it's mine."

I'm going to miss this? I'm going to miss hearing adolescents who are supposed to love each other shout, "You jerk," "You loser!" "Fang Face!" and "Oh, yeah? Well at least I don't look like a tin can?"

I'm going to miss conversations full of "So he goes, 'Really?' and I go, 'I was just kiddin?' "

I'm going to miss, "There's nothing to eat," "We need a ride to the movies," "There's nothing to do-oo," ice trays that are always empty, a sink that is always full, Coke cans everywhere, wet towels on the floor, incessant music, constant chatter, interminable noise?

Yes, I'm going to miss it all. The quarrels, the mess, the sounds. I love summer, I love having my children home, I love reclaiming what was mine originally, what the world takes away every September and returns in a bigger size every June — a little smarter, a little more independent, a little less mine.

Summer is my sustenance. My skin breathes in the sun and the air and my heart takes in my children. They warm me. They sustain me, and though sometimes their actions burn and their words hurt, their presence is a joy.

I'm going to miss this constant exposure. I'm going to miss watching horror movies with them, having long talks that come easier in the night when there's no homework, no school the next day.

I'm going to miss mornings that stretch like saltwater taffy into evenings nearly as sweet. I'm even going to miss the noise, the music, the squeak of the refrigerator door, mustard on the counter, potato chips on the floor. Everything. I wish summer could last forever, I tell my daughter who sits beside me, the basketball now returned to her brother.

"It wouldn't be so special then," she says. "You'd get sick of it. And you'd get sick of us."

No, I wouldn't.

Already I am mourning summer's passing. September lurks in the shadows. I have seen it, in the moss green of trees, in the smell of early morning, when its presence is assaulting, the way the aroma of steak sizzling on a grill sometimes floods a car passing by. Already the air tingles with fall. And I am tinged with regret.

Oh, but September is a beginning, people tell me. It's a wonderful time of year. I suppose it is. For children. After all, they count their lives in Septembers. New clothes, new friends. First grade, fourth grade, high school, college. Turn around and they're tiny, turn around and they're grown.

And then? Then it stops and September is no longer a beginning but an end. The end of vacation. The end of shorts and bare feet. The end of sleeping on top of the covers, of being happy with slushes and banana popsicles and macaroni salad and corn on the cob.

September's the end of open windows and open minds, of deciding at 10 p.m. that an ice cream would be wonderful and not hesitating before racing to the car. September's the end of late-night movies, reading until dawn, listening to birds and crickets, the end of barbecues and baseball and beer.

In September people become sensible again, donning responsibility along with sweaters still creased from the drawer. Options diminish, the calendar intrudes and the days contract like a purse being cinched until suddenly there is no more time to sip coffee and read the morning newspaper outdoors because someone needs breakfast, or something ironed, or a ride to school.

We'll be inside working, attending to business we've let slip all summer, straightening out our lives and our homes and September will steal the heat and the flowers and our children and it will do so with flair, in a burst of colors so bright, so beautiful we won't even know it's happening until the heat and the flowers and our children are gone. The trees will be bare and summer a memory before we notice.

So during these final days of summer I will cling. I will hold on to the magic just a little longer. I will take my children back-to-school shopping. We will swim, and we will stay up late and watch movies and talk and forget that September is waiting. This is the last dance.

But we won't quit until the music stops.

The First Day of School

Thursday, September 4, 1975

Yesterday, Robbie started school. I watched him swagger down the front walk and struggle up the steps of the bus and I felt suddenly replaceable. I have such a feeling of emptiness without him now that he is no longer dependent upon me. He never looked back, never waved goodbye. He was so eager to leave, I wonder if I really made use of the time we've had together or if, too often, I pushed him aside for something else. That part of him that was exclusively mine for six years I'll never have again. I never realized letting go could hurt so much.

Lauren is home and floundering, too. I'm sure we'll adjust in time, but today I feel an inestimable loss.

September 7, 1977

I am wretched today. I'd just become used to Robbie's being away at school all day and now it's Lauren's turn. I know she's ready and has been looking forward to it. But am I ready? That's the question. They're both growing up too fast. At least there's still Julie. It will be years before she's in school.

September 7, 1983

The years have passed. Where did they go? I no longer keep a journal. I no longer write down my thoughts. Yet because of sentimental words scrawled in pen nearly a decade ago, the past appears today, untouched by reverie.

I am embarrassed by the intensity of my feelings. I know that if I hadn't written them out, corroborated them with nouns and adjectives and verbs, I could deny ever having had them. I could tell myself that memory plays tricks, that time exaggerates everything. That I never had that much difficulty letting go. But I did. My journal won't let me lie.

In later entries, I described changes in my son and daughter. I wrote about how school affected them. I can see now that the changes were mostly positive, the effects good. What I anticipated — not being needed anymore — never happened. It seems, in fact, that as they grew older they needed me in different ways, less physically and more psychologically.

I take solace in this because today my baby started school. My baby. I used to cringe when women referred to their youngest child as their "baby." But that was before I realized that we say the word to deny the truth of their growing, to hang on just a little longer to the myth that these children of ours are still small and dependent.

"She won't be starting school until Robbie's a freshman," I used to say smugly, the way when I was young I would calculate that in the year 2000 I would be 53. It was a trick of numbers and numbers didn't mean anything because it would never be the year 2000 and I would never be 53 and Robbie would never start high school and Julie would never grow up.

Today I walk around, swallowing hard, humming "Sunrise, Sunset," wondering how it is possible to spend 24 hours a day with a child and not notice that she's grown.

"Someday you're going to grow up and leave me," my mother said to me.

"I'll never leave you, Mommy," I promised.

"Yes, you will. All children grow up and leave their mothers. You'll get a job and move far away or you'll get married. You'll leave. The same way I left my mother, you'll leave me. It happens."

"Not me. I'm never leaving. I'm going to live here and

take care of you forever."

My mother just smiled. She knew. We all leave.

We leave in increments, the leaving like aging — slow, almost imperceptible. It comes upon us like our reflection in a shop window, suddenly, dramatically, and we are left wondering when? When did the change take place? When did the aging happen? When did it start?

It starts, I think, in first grade. School is the initial installment in growing up, in growing old.

The night before school this year, I bathed my small daughter, layed out her clothes and kissed her goodnight, all without tears.

And in the morning, my eyes did not betray my feelings when I saw her clutching Teddy in one hand and her Smurf school bag in the other.

"Are you excited about school?" I asked, snapping her picture on the front walk, a picture to be added to the scrapbook where her brother and sister smile out at me from the same front walk, frozen forever at six.

"Not really," she sighed.

"Are you going to take Teddy?"

"No. I just didn't want him sitting alone upstairs all day. He'll be lonely."

"I'll be lonely, too. We'll keep each other company."

"Okay," she nodded.

As the bus lumbered to a stop I kissed her goodbye. She skipped down the walk swinging her bag and struggled up the steps just like her brother and sister before her. She didn't look back either. She didn't wave goodbye. But this time I didn't cry. I know she's not gone forever. She'll be home at three o'clock.

And Teddy and I will be waiting for her.

Never Too Late For Kids

O h, if you could see him...

His eyes shine. His skin glows. He grins constantly. Plus he struts. Yes, the man struts. He holds his head just a little lower than the clouds, squares his shoulders and struts — jaunty, eager, proud steps — like a man who has fallen in love.

I suppose in a way he has.

"She's the best looking baby who's ever been born! No doubt about it. None at all."

From the second he knew about her, he changed. Conversations full of layouts and designs, meetings he'd attended, golf games he'd played, began to meander to stories about morning sickness and weight gain in pregnancy. "The doctor said there was nothing to worry about, but she should watch her weight." "The doctor said next month she'll be able to hear the baby's heartbeat."

In nine months, the unflappable executive became impassioned about childbirth. Words like amniocentesis, placenta praevia, ultrasound and fetal monitor rolled off his tongue as easily as pagination and computer printout. He became personally involved in the pregnancy. He knew the size of the fetus at every stage; he knew what organs were developing; he could debate the advantages of natural childbirth versus spinals and epidurals.

For nearly the entire pregnancy, the man was deliriously happy. Only at the end did he worry, when the doctor said there might be a problem. The baby wasn't in position. The baby wasn't dropping. It was time, and the baby wasn't ready to be born. A Caesarean might be necessary.

"Don't worry," women who had had babies told him. "Doctors don't know everything. The baby will be born when it's good and ready to be born."

But he continued to frown.

He was at work when it happened. The phone rang and a happy, tired voice said, "Dad? Dad? You have a granddaughter."

A granddaughter. A little girl. His own grandchild.

After he asked: Are you all right? Is she all right? Who does she look like? After he oohed and aahed, and gasped and cried; after he sat at his desk for a while, alone, quietly taking in the fact that his baby had had a baby; after his brain acknowledged it and his heart reveled in it; after all this, he stood up, and he was taller than he'd ever been — inches, feet, yards taller.

He flew to Florida to see this baby. He spent his vacation there watching her, holding her, listening to her giggle and gurgle, stealing her away from his daughter and his son-in-law and his wife every chance he could. "She gained a half a pound while I was there," he declared when he arrived home, the weight tangible proof of his love.

Now he calls every day. "She didn't sleep well last night. She isn't eating enough. Kathy's going to try giving her supplementary bottles," he declares, over a cup of coffee.

Supplementary bottles.

When his own children were babies, he didn't know these words. He didn't know the difference between the first trimester and the last trimester. The birth of his children was a mystery to him. He wasn't allowed to take part. He wasn't invited to the doctor's, to childbirth classes, to the delivery room.

Then, after they were born, when they were infants and toddlers, he worked two jobs, 16-, 18- and 20-hour days. He would creep in at night, tiptoe into their room and kiss their tiny heads. In the morning, he would peek in again, kissing them once more before he left for work. But he wasn't home to feed them. He wasn't home to tuck them into bed. He didn't have the time to spend with them or the luxury of holding them.

They were grown before he did.

Now he is a grandfather and he has the time.

So he's phoning ("She cooed to me today. She probably knew it was her grandfather.") and watching home videos, ("Look at that baby? Isn't she beautiful?") and showing off the latest snapshots ("Have you ever seen a prettier child? Tell the truth, now. Isn't she a love?") and planning a winter vacation.

And, of course, he's still strutting. You might have seen him. Ten feet tall. A grin on his face. A bounce in his step. His head in the clouds.

Just a typical grandfather, that's what he is, thrilled and smitten, and proud of it.

You Can't Go Back

I saw the movie days ago, but the mood still lingers, clings really, like the angel hair Rosemary's mother used to put on her Christmas tree. Rose and I would be playing — dolls or jacks or hide-and-seek — weeks, sometimes months, after the tree had been thrown away, and find a stray strand of the shimmery stuff, hugging the side of the couch, hiding in a skein of wool, poking up from under a rug. The discovery would take us back to caroling, and watching "The Littlest Angel" at the Baptist church, and opening a huge pile of gifts. It would make us remember, make us yearn, even, for that special day that seemed so far away.

Yes, the feeling is like angel hair, full of memory and hope and even regret, brought on this time not by some remnant of Christmas but by a movie, "Peggy Sue Got Married."

In the story a woman whose marriage is on the rocks, whose world is falling apart, arrives at her 25th reunion, regretting the way her life has turned out. But, with the wave of Hollywood's magic wand, the years retreat like soldiers deserting a lost cause and Peggy Sue becomes young again, with the chance to do it all over, to change the course of her life.

It's a wonderful fantasy, isn't it? Play it again, Sam, only differently, flawlessly, this time with the wisdom of an adult.

The movie focuses primarily on Peggy Sue's relationship with her boyfriend/husband. But it is in the random glimpses of ordinary life — when Peggy Sue finds herself back in the room in which she grew up, when she looks at her mother and says, "I never remembered you so young," when she talks to her grandmother for a final time — that the film becomes more than a series of images on a screen.

For the fact is, we all ache to go back. We try to, every day, in small ways. The old songs, the new cars, the stacks of pictures, the saved letters, the trips back home, the traditions, the reunions, the "remember whens?"

"If you could relive any 24 hours of your life, which would they be?" I have asked people, and always the answers are varied. "I'd want to be a senior in high school again. That was the happiest time of my life."

"I'd go back to the moment my son was born. Nothing has ever come close to the way I felt then."

"I'd go back to my wedding day."

"I'd go back to the day I met my wife."

"I'd go home and see my mother."

It is perhaps our greatest curse, that as human beings we are like trees, stuck in one place at one time. We can't travel through the years the way we travel through space. We are rooted solidly in the here and now.

A husband and wife sit across the table from one another and have nothing to say. Once they couldn't stop talking. Once they tied up the phone long into the night.

A father doesn't speak to his son. Though on the day that son was born he swore he wouldn't be like his father — cold, unbending, unforgiving.

A mother shuns her mother. "When you get old, I'll take care of you," she used to say. But she doesn't remember.

None of these people remembers. They see only the now, the past buried under an accumulation of years and worries and disappointments. But if they could go back? If, for an hour, for a day, they could see themselves and each other as they once were?

"What color hair did you have when you were born?" my nine-year-old asks her grandmother. "What color hair did you have when you started school? When you came to America? When you got married?"

"Why do you care what color hair Grandma had?" her older sister snaps.

"Because I can't imagine Grandma as anything but Grandma. I can't picture her as a kid, like me."

"I used to be a kid like you," Grandma says. "I had blonde hair and every morning before I went to school my mother would comb it and wrap it around her fingers and make curls like this." And she twirls a few strands of hair around her finger.

My daughter studies her and sighs. She cannot believe in the child underneath the white hair and the soft lap and the comforting arms. Despite the words and the pictures and the, "Look, see that's me, right there," she cannot imagine Grandma as anyone but Grandma.

And that's the pity. We burst into someone's life, walk with him a while, then move on ahead, or drop behind, never really knowing who he was or who he'll become because we haven't been there from the beginning and we don't know if we'll get to stay for the end.

For life is a play, not a movie. You miss an act and it's gone. There's no rewind button. You get one chance and one chance only.

And so we go to the movies and yearn.

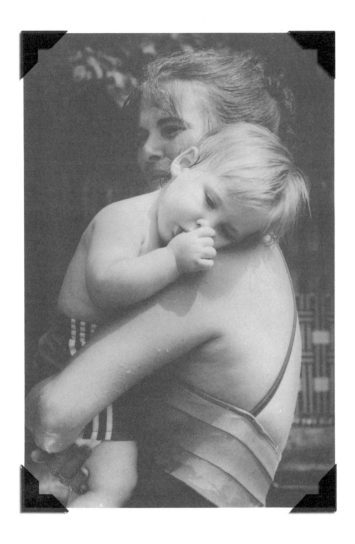

The Glossing of the Past

My brain urged me not to go. It reminded me of the years I'd spent locking the door on my adolescence. "Forgotten what it was like?" it sneered. "Then step this way and take a look."

There it was. The past. The girl I was, fuzzy-haired, wide-hipped, squeezed into a plaid skirt and navy blazer, quarreling with an isosceles triangle. Embarrassed by my ignorance, my hair, my entire being.

"You daydream too much. You'll never get to college. Why don't you pay attention!" Sister screamed.

"I will. I'll change. I'm sorry." Wanting to die. To have the world devour me and spit me out somewhere else.

But I didn't die nor did I change. For four years I daydreamed through math and science wishing I were someone else, someone smarter, brighter. Someone popular. I would have sold my soul for popular.

The invitation to the reunion brought it all back. All the insecurity. All the pain. Did I really want an evening of being 14 again?

Once before we'd gathered together, 10 years after graduation, and it had been an extension of high school. Instead of uniforms we wore suits and gowns. Instead of asking "What are you doing this weekend?" we said, "What do you do?"

We dangled our husbands and wives, pictures of our children and our successes the way we used to hang crosses from our neck — for all the world to see. Our conversations were as lusterless and artificial as the polyesters we wore. Why would I want to go to another reunion? Did I really need to disturb a past I'd prefer to forget?

Why, indeed. Curiosity, maybe? A belief that this time things would be different?

Well, this time things were different. This time we met, not as people intent upon impressing one another but as veterans, soldiers who'd fought in the same battle and had won a war. The atmosphere had changed. The question asked was no longer "What do you do?" but "How are you?" There was affection and caring and, when one recognized a familiar face, a kind of joy.

The music played, supposedly records from the '60s, but the disc jockey was young, so Willie Nelson sang instead. But it didn't matter because the past was happening inside us. And it was a past without jagged edges, made tender by the years the way a rock is made smooth by the sea.

Adults — married, single, some living miles from where they grew up, some still close to home — were connected by a bond that hadn't existed before. If it had, it was perceived as a noose because it forced us all to be the same.

The boys had crew cuts then, and the girls teased their hair and rolled up their skirts. We all tried to blend in because we didn't want to be singled out, at the board, at a dance, anywhere. "Yes, Sister. No, Sister. Please don't look at me, Sister." Every day, praying to be ignored. Every night, hoping to be noticed.

Now — because we are older? Because we're less afraid of being different? Because few links are as strong as four years of saying the rosary in unison every morning? — there was a feeling among us that hadn't existed before.

The feeling — more honest than nostalgia, stronger than camaraderie, more intense than shared experience — was a gift of four hours in which to walk through the corridors of high school without fear of not belonging.

You see, the night of the reunion, everyone belonged. We were all 14 again and everyone spoke. Everyone reminisced and there was no one who didn't fit in. For the rules had changed. The differences we once perceived as flaws didn't count anymore. Too tall, too short, too smart, too shy, he doesn't like me, she doesn't care, no longer mattered. We were ourselves without apology. And what we found that evening was what we'd sought 20 years before: Acceptance.

Live For The Day

Johnny Mason had been telling his wife the same thing for years: "I just don't have the time now, May. We'll go next year for sure. I promise."

And every year as the green of spring inched its way through the still-frozen ground, as summer coaxed the heather to bright purple in the countryside, Johnny would look toward America, toward his dream. "Next year, for sure," he'd vow. "Next year for sure."

They had almost made it a couple of times. A travel agent was consulted, brochures inspected, trans-Atlantic telephone calls made to friends.

But a problem developed at work and Johnny had to cancel his vacation. Once his mother was hospitalized; then his kids were sick or involved in activities and leaving them was impossible. Always, reasons existed for his not leaving home.

"We just don't have the time," the letters apologized year after year. "But someday we will. Someday we'll get there."

Someday never came for Johnny Mason. One morning a few years ago, he awoke with a stiff neck and a throbbing headache. By mid-afternoon, he was in the hospital, paralyzed by a stroke.

For months, he fought to recover the good health he had taken for granted. And a funny thing happened: Life went on without him. His business survived. So did his mother. Even his children adjusted to life without father, finding rides to movies and dances, existing, even flourishing, despite his absence.

Johnny Mason never recovered and died without ever visiting America.

"It was something he always dreamed of," May wrote in the letter about his death. "He should have made the time. Now it's too late."

Time. Hands on a clock. Days in a week. Squares on a calendar. Props created for our convenience. Harness time and we might be able to understand and control it. But we don't. It controls us.

Tick-tock; tick-tock. Spring, summer, fall and winter. Our lives are metered out in seasons and decades and life spans, cluttered with birthdays and anniversaries and commitments. And we stick dutifully to our schedules like tongues to dry ice because to pull away would be painful.

So we say, "I'm sorry I haven't seen you, but I'll give you a call," or "I'd love to come by, but who has the time?" and "Sure, we'll get together soon, you'll see."

And the years go by and the children grow up and we grow old, time rushing by like whitewater, pushing us along cruelly, quickly, without consent, forcing us into middle age, into old age, into bodies too old for our minds, into wheelchairs and rest homes, into our graves.

At any moment it might stop, this experience we call life, because it is just a sophisticated game of "Beat the Clock" and we are all reluctant players, all losers in a game no one can win.

So why don't we make the most of life while we're here? While we have time? Why do we live life marginally, saving the best — all our cherished dreams — for a day that might never come?

"You're a long time dead," my father always says philosophically when I give him a list of reasons why I can't go somewhere or do something. "Opportunities don't come along every day. It's up to you to take every moment, every experience, and make the best of it. Use it. Learn from it."

I used to think my father was wrong; I don't anymore.

Intellectually we know that we won't be here forever. But emotionally, we don't seem to comprehend this. So we postpone our trips, our family outings, our visits with friends because we are responsible, sensible people with commitments. We are indispensable. We do not indulge in frivolities.

Instead, we wish our lives away, imagining the day we can buy the boat we've always wanted, take the trip we've planned a hundred times.

But one day you wake up and you don't feel too well. You're a little short of breath or your legs are stiff or your eyes don't focus quite as they should. A few days later you go to the doctor and he recommends a hospital stay.

And amazingly, your boss gets along without you, someone else feeds the cat and the world goes on spinning. You realize then you could have fulfilled your dream. But now it's too late.

"Someday, when my ship comes in," my mother used to sigh when I asked her why she never went anywhere, why she never did anything exciting. And I, a child, imagined that somewhere in the mid-Atlantic was a pirate vessel adrift without a compass, heavy with jewels and treasure chests belonging to us, but inaccessible.

"Someday, when the kids are older," I hear now. "When the house is paid for, when the weather breaks, I'll take that trip, go back to school, join a club, write all those letters."

It's the same tune we all sing generation after generation. Only the lyrics change. We are all Johnny Masons living our lives on the deferment plan as if tomorrow were the play and today simply the dress rehearsal. And what happens as we postpone, as we practice for the ultimate performance, is that we lose the audience, our own little grandstand of spectators who have witnessed and shared our lives. They move away. They die. Their time runs out.

Reversing Roles

"W hy are you going out again? Can't I come with you? I don't want you to go. I want you to stay home with me."

Words of love from my 10-year-old.

My older children used to say the same things, used to cry when they were babies, when I would leave them for an evening; used to beg, when they grew older, to tag along wherever I'd go.

"We'll be good. We won't make any noise. We promise." Sometimes their demands would annoy me. Why couldn't they stay home with someone else for a while. The things I had to do weren't fun things. Alone I could finish more quickly and get home sooner, and then play with them.

I tried reasoning, explaining. "But we want to be with you," they insisted.

So they came. Everywhere. To the grocery store, the bank, the library, the movies. Anywhere I went, there they were, right by my side.

Most times I didn't mind, but there were days I ached for moments alone. Driving in the car, I would turn on the radio and a song would come on, one that I loved and I'd turn up the volume and a little voice would interrupt. "What does 'Go Children Slow' mean, Mommy?" "What town are we in?" "Did I tell you what happened yesterday?" And the song would be long over by the time the story was told.

In restaurants, I'd be listening to a friend, hoping my son and daughter would talk to each other, which they did. They always tried to be polite. But there were important questions, legitimate interruptions. "Mommy, do they put celery in the egg salad in this place?" "Can I have a vanilla milk shake?" "Will you go to the bathroom with me?" And I'd wish for a time when I could finish a sentence, have a complete thought, eat one entire meal without interruption.

It was my attention they wanted. My opinion and presence they craved. I was the audience they played to day after day. I became accustomed to their stories, their interruptions. Their fresh observations enriched me. "Why is that man called a waiter, Mom, when we're the ones doing the waiting?" "How come the sign says 'dressing room' when everyone goes in to undress?"

As they grew older, their questions became less entertaining and more annoying. The early teen-age years were accompanied by a litany of demands and complaints. "How come everyone else can go out on school nights and I can't?" "No one else has to be home by 11 o'clock. Don't you trust me?"

Then, most of all, I wished they would be quiet, find something else to do, someone else to listen to them. Why did even the simplest things have to turn into confrontations? Couldn't they ever just leave me alone?

Now, too often, they do.

"How was your day?" I'll ask my 17-year-old son, when he comes home from work. "Where did you go? What did you do?"

"We hung doors somewhere. It was no big deal, Mom. It was just work."

Just work. This isn't fair. I want detail. I want texture. I want to know what he does 12 hours a day. I want to hear about his friends, listen to his stories.

"How was your trip, Mom? What did you see? Did you have fun?" he used to ask only a few years ago. "What did you do at night? Did you go out? Did you miss us?" The endless questions always answered, always explained.

"Are you going out again tonight?" I find myself saying.

"Can't you stay home sometime? You'll be leaving for college in three weeks and I already miss you now."

Why didn't someone tell me this was going to happen? Everything is reversed. Now I'm the one tagging along, saying, "I miss you." "When are you coming home?" Marking it on the calendar when he has a day off.

Mornings when I drive my daughter to work, if a song she likes comes on the radio, she turns up the volume and I know better than to talk. She loses herself in the music. She doesn't want to hear what I have to say. And I understand.

But underneath the understanding, there's this feeling, this growing awakening: This is how she felt, how my son felt years ago. Afraid that something — some song, some play, some activity, some person — would come along and take me away from them. She shouldn't like that song more than she likes me, a child thinks. She shouldn't be able to have fun without me. So the child complains and the child imposes. Here I am. Look at me.

Here I am. Look at me, this adult wants to say. But of course I don't. I simply understand a little better when my 10-year-old sulks when I am someplace she can't be. Finally, after all these years, I am beginning to understand why children cry when they are left behind.

Mothers and Daughters

I don't know much about Ruthie. I don't even know her last name. We met a year ago when my mother and her mother shared a hospital room. Over the years I've met a lot of people in hospital rooms, a lot of daughters tending to their mothers, but I've never met anyone quite like Ruthie.

What struck me the first time I saw her was how hard she tried, how much effort she expended attempting to make her mother happy.

Once, about eight years ago at Carney Hospital, there was another daughter who tried almost as hard, who appeared every day at her mother's side carrying flowers and a cake, bringing stories about the outside world, saying "Hi Mom, how are you doing?" fluffing up her pillow, bending over to kiss her mother's pinched, unyielding cheek.

And the old woman, who snapped at the nurses and called the hospital food garbage and all the doctors quacks, would glare at this daughter and scream, "Why do you continue to waste your money on flowers and cake? What are you trying to do, poison me? Don't you know I don't give a damn about your daughter and her prom? Why don't you just go away and leave me alone?"

And the younger woman would break then, bowing her head, excusing herself, running down the corridor, weeping.

I never saw Ruthie cry. Ruthie's mother wasn't critical. She never said the food was lousy or "I wish you'd go away."

Ruthie's mother never yelled and screamed. Ruthie's mother never said a word. But her eyes accused Ruthie of terrible things, of putting her in this place, of allowing the tubes and the pain and the constant humiliation. And Ruthie's mother's silence was as sharp and as critical as the other woman's complaints.

Still Ruthie tried. I've never seen anyone try so hard. She

worked every day, getting up at 4:30 in the morning to open a donut shop where she stood on her feet for 10, sometimes 12 hours at a time, pouring coffee and listening to other people's troubles. I have the feeling Ruthie never let on that she had troubles of her own. I never once heard her complain on the long afternoons I saw her when she would appear at the door of the hospital room, still dressed in her uniform, smelling like coffee, carrying two fresh cups for my mother and me.

Her mother couldn't have coffee or donuts or any outside food so Ruthie always brought a helium balloon or a stuffed animal or a card from a friend. And the mother would look at it the way she looked at the nurse who checked her blood pressure and the aide who brought her food — the way she looked at Ruthie — as if nothing and no one meant anything at all.

Once Ruthie told me about a man she had loved and how it hadn't worked out. But mostly she talked to my children about their friends and their lives, always including her mother in the conversations. "Did you hear that, Mom? So what do you think?"

Ruthie was like a cheerleader, determined to rally a losing team.

Ruthie's mother got a little better and eventually went home and another woman took her place in my mother's room and time passed. I stopped once in a while at the donut store to say hi to Ruthie and to get coffee for my mother, but then my mother was transferred and I didn't see Ruthie anymore.

But a few days ago I was driving by the donut store and decided to stop. I walked in expecting to see Ruthie, expecting her to tell me her mother had died. She was busy, waiting on a counter full of people, and at first she didn't remember me.

"Our mothers were in the hospital together," I explained.

She looked tired and had trouble focusing on last February as if there had been too many months filled with too many days all like last February. "My mother's in a nursing home," she told me. "I still feed her dinner every night."

I cried on the way home, not because Ruthie's mother is in a nursing home and not because Ruthie looked tired and worn out. I cried for all the Ruthies who every day visit their mothers, and hold their hands and brush their hair and tell them stories about old friends and whisper encouragement, ministering to them, consoling them, loving them, even when their mothers are silent and weak, and either cannot or pretend not to love them back.

I cried because these are good people trying to do the right thing. Life is so tough sometimes, and it isn't easy watching someone you love, someone you remember as a whole living, loving human being die slowly, like a puzzle being taken apart, one piece at a time.

Indian Summer

The day begs attention. I sit at my desk and try to concentrate but my eyes keep drifting to the window and the world outside and eventually lead me there, the morning too rich to ignore.

It is a different world today, warm and soft and glazed with a thin layer of sunshine, November in name only. There is no breeze, so the leaves on the ground are silent and the shadows are still, and if it weren't for the occasional leaf floating noiselessly by, I could believe that the world is a backdrop, so clean and clear it seems outlined, the way a child darkens the edges of a picture he has colored.

It seems a shame that no one is outside. That here is all this beauty, a once in a lifetime performance put on by Mother Nature, and the house is empty, the audience somewhere else.

Maybe it's our city mentality. It's difficult driving to and from work, over highways and crowded streets, on buses and subways to consider glens and dales, since they don't exist here anymore. We have to visit them on weekends, at theme parks and recreated villages. We have to make plans to take the time to see.

On normal days, we're too busy. Responsibility prevails. Everyone is working, hustling, racing, running. Our back yards are empty and spontaneity is dead. And here is the world in all its glory, a gift in the middle of the week, in the middle of a month that is usually gray and dull and ugly, and if we get to appreciate it for a minute, we're lucky.

The weather man predicted this day. A touch of Indian summer, he said on the evening news, the phrase reminiscent of harvests and feasts and the lasts days of summer, the words filling my head with a dozen images, real and imagined, all intertwined like chips of color in a kaleidoscope.

I remember the first time I heard them spoken together, in

school, in Miss Nagel's class. She called Indian summer beautiful, opening the fire escape door in the converted building that served as a school for two classes of fifth graders. I remember how the warmth spilling in lured her, lured us, into going outside to sit under a tree while she told us tales of Indians and corn and shoring up for the winter; and I remember how we all sang in our loudest voices, Thanksgiving songs of praise.

I remember a different Indian summer in the eighth grade, when the Monsignor strode into class one November afternoon, surprising us and Sister, too, by announcing in a voice kinder than we had ever heard, that the next day would be a holiday because God didn't mean for us to be inside when He'd wrapped the world in such beauty.

No holidays were ever given later, in high school or in college or in adult life. Moments had to be stolen, and were, in missed classes and pilfered days, in afternoons when, as a teacher, I'd lead a fourth grade class outdoors to sing songs and later, as a mother, phone the school and say that someone had a dentist appointment because the world was too beautiful for my own children to miss.

The effort was always worth the deceit. Indian summer is a visitor who knocks at your door when you're too busy for company, when you don't have time, when you least expect it, but who disappears if you waver, who is gone before the kettle boils, who is whisked away by a gust of wind even as you watch.

Indian summer lingers today. I open my office window and the leaves that blow in sound like a girl dressed in taffeta. I think there's a party going without me and I hurry, so that the celebration won't end without my farewell.

That it will end is inevitable. Everything does. Except

memory. Memory, like Indian summer, is another gift.

"God gave us our memories so that we might have roses in December," Sir James Barrie wrote.

And He gave us Indian summer so we might have memories all winter long.

She's off to College

So it isn't just me. I was beginning to believe this was over-reaction of the worst kind. My daughter is leaving for college in a few weeks, a perfectly natural next step in her life. She is not leaving for boot camp or to fight a war. She does not have an incurable disease; she is not running away from home or getting married. She is simply going to school, growing up, moving on. I am happy for her, but incredibly sad for me.

The sadness is selfish; I have hidden it well. I don't look sad or act sad. I walk around pretending that everything's fine, that sending my oldest daughter off to school is the most natural thing in the world. Look at all the people who've been through this and survived, I think. It can't be that bad.

Then I remember a younger me, breathing easily in Lamaze class, panting, smiling, relaxing between fake contractions, sure that childbirth would be bearable, too. Look at all the people who have had babies, I used to think. It can't be that bad. Then the real labor started and breathing didn't help and neither did the panting, so I screamed and cried through it, not just because of the pain, but because I realized that all of the people had lied.

Are they lying now? Is this another one of those secrets you don't tell people because eventually they find out for themselves? What is it like when your daughter doesn't live at home anymore? I've been through this with a son and though that first September was awful, October was better and by November he was home. Then he returned often on weekends and during semester break and soon it was May. Looking back now I can say the letting go wasn't as difficult as I'd expected.

But this is my oldest daughter, the one who brings home school stories and work stories and thoughts and ideas I remember from my own youth; the one who likes old movies and sits and watches them with me, then makes me watch MTV so I'll know what is going on in her world. This is the one who tells me when clothes don't match, then drags me shopping so she can pick out clothes that do match. This is the one who is more than a daughter, the one who is also my friend.

When my best friend and I went to different high schools our mothers assured us that we would still be close. We would see each other on weekends. We would see each other on school vacations and all summer long. Nothing would change, they said.

But everything changed. Rose went her way and I went mine.

Is that what will happen now? Is this an inevitable closing of the doors that took years to open? When my daughter was 14 and wretched, I didn't think we would ever be friends. We couldn't spend more than five minutes in the same room without quarreling.

Now we never quarrel. We like each other. We seek each other out. Will this change? Will distance force us apart?

"I don't know what I am going to do without her," a woman I had never met before was saying at a cocktail party last week, saying out loud the very words I have been thinking. She had returned the day before from Florida, from getting her daughter settled at a college there.

"She called last night and we talked a half hour and she's doing fine, really she is. It's me I'm worried about. When we hung up all I could do was cry. I miss her so much already."

Her tears are selfish ones, I know, because my sadness is selfish, too. But imagine devoting 18 years to something and then walking away. Imagine spending 18 years at anything, only to let it go.

Kings of the Hill

He came home for the weekend, the college freshman, carrying his dirty laundry stuffed into a garbage bag ("I've got a present for you, Mom"), the smile on his face so huge and relaxed that "How's school?" didn't need to be asked.

He was great. School was great. Life was great. He sauntered into the family room, sprawled on the couch and endured our eager and assorted questions. "Did you miss me, Bro?"

"I missed you, Brain," he said to his little sister.

"When are you gonna invite me up to visit?" his other sister asked.

"Maybe next month," he said.

"What are your classes like? Is it hard? Do you like your teachers?"

He fielded questions with adult deference, pacifying instead of antagonizing as he might have just a few months before, as he has all of his life, answering each as if it were the only question. He was a king home from the hunt, and we were eager to listen to tales of his adventures, curious to know all about this new life which didn't include us.

His friends stopped by, other college freshmen home for the holiday, who in September went away tentatively, shyly, untried kites being let out slowly, held taut by worried mothers and fathers, soaring now, buoyed by a current that was self-created, elevated by their own new, rising confidence.

They walked taller, these boys who looked more mature than their high school pictures. They spoke with authority and ease. They should have. They earned this right, having gone out and made friends and survived in a place all by themselves, most for the first time in their lives.

No mothers were there reminding, "Did you finish your homework? Have you had breakfast?" No fathers were demanding that the TV be shut off, that they put down the hockey stick or the basketball and hit the books and study. Only their own young voices guided them. And their voices have guided them well.

Peter, just a boy when he left for Tucson, showed us pictures of his girlfriend. "She's beautiful," we said. "I know," he replied in a man's voice, in a tone no longer full of question marks. Yes, he was doing well in school, and yes, he was happy in his fraternity and no, he hardly missed home at all. Danny, Mike, Frank, they all said the same things, all comfortable in their expanded lives, in the realization that they can and have made it alone.

I watched all weekend, and listened, not just to what was said but to how it was said, and realized that for these new freshmen, this was a moment of perfect happiness.

I wished I had a magic wand so I could have waved it over these boys, so I could make the moment last forever. It won't, of course. There will be doubt and setbacks and ambivalence. Still, there will always be the memory of this one weekend when the high school boys they were met the men they are becoming for the first time.

That Old House

I was six years old when I stood beside my mother and father on a soggy patch of land gazing at fresh foundations and a few bulldozers at work.

"This is ours," my mother announced, counting the steps from where our front yard would be to the end of the muddy lot. "All this is ours."

I can picture her — hiking up her dress, wiping mud from her black high heels. I can hear the wonder in her voice, the eagerness transcending time.

A home in the country — my mother's dream. Years of two jobs and a GI loan enabled us to move from Somerville to Randolph. City mice used to subways and Central Square, we became the proud occupants of an unfinished cape in the winter of '54, adjusting quickly to life in suburbia.

My father bought a hammer, nails and a "Handyman for Novices" book and converted the house's empty spaces into two bedrooms, a study and an elaborate "whoopy room."

My mother planted bachelor buttons and rose bushes around a massive boulder the builder had hidden under rubble in the backyard. "It'll make a lovely rock garden," he assured her when, dismayed, she called to complain. Always naive, she ended up thanking him for his suggestion.

My childhood is inextricably bound to that inanimate mixture of cement and plaster and wood upon which my parents pinned their highest expectations.

A few years ago, my father sold the house. Since then, I've driven past it regularly. Sometimes I look at the trees grown tall and thick, admire the paint or the awnings, gaze at the walkway edged in flowers. But mostly I drive by simply to remember.

* * *

"When I was a kid, banana splits cost 50 cents," I tell my son as we wait in line at the Dairy Queen. I am giving him another grand tour of Randolph by twilight. I conduct this tour sporadically and spontaneously, bribing potential patrons with the promise of an ice cream cone the size of their choice. This time my son is the only taker.

"I know, Mom. You've told me a hundred times," he moans.

I continue my reverie, undaunted, borrowing from John Irving's "The Hotel New Hampshire." "For half your life you're fifteen. Then one day your twenties begin and they're over the next day. And your thirties blow by you like a weekend spent with pleasant company. And before you know it you're thinking about being fifteen again."

My son stares at me strangely.

I want to be 15 again. I want to go home, slip inside the safety of the house that was my refuge. I want to knock on the door, middle age and my almost-teenage son my companions, and step, however briefly, into a childhood that is still precious to me.

"This used to be a dirt road," I explain traveling down High Street, my unsolicited recitation of life in the '60s familiar to my son. "The piggery was over there," I point. "There weren't any street lights and right there, where the buses are parked, is where we used to go parking."

"You went parking, Mom?" he chides. He thinks this is the best part of the true but tired story.

Today, High Street looks like Central Square, all concrete and offices and condominiums. The city mice have taken over the country.

We approach my old house slowly, the car comfortable in first gear. The lights are on inside and hospitality beckons.

"Come with me?" I ask my son, curiosity and need overriding my palpable unease.

Together we walk up the front steps, where I posed dozens of times. "Smile for the camera, honey," at First Communion, each September on the first day of school, as a Brownie, a Girl Scout, for proms and graduation, and for the final time as a bride, my hand tucked inside my father's.

"No suffering is greater than remembering happy times," the ancient Greeks proclaimed.

I ring the bell. The new owner comes to the door. She is gracious and understanding and invites us in.

The house has changed. It wears a wardrobe chosen by strangers. The kitchen is no longer red; the dining room no longer. Upstairs, the tree that terrified me nightly with its outstretched tentacles has grown fat and docile, a tired-out monster.

Outside, where Rose and I performed summer talent shows, the patio has been resurfaced, our family name buried under inches of new cement.

The clothesline is gone, the trees grown together, the flowers lush around the unsightly boulder.

I expected something different? A household of old tunes, my father's voice, my mother's laugh? I expected the past in 35 mm slides to be laid out before me in Kodacolor? I expected a child in a red cotton dress with a red ribbon pinned to her hair to embrace me, to recognize me as herself in a bigger size?

The house has changed, as I have changed. We have both matured and endured. I glimpse impressions of what used to be — in the familiar woodwork, stained by my father; in the closet, the same now as when my mother's clothes hung there; in the knick-knack shelf still unprotected by glass. I recognize the unchanged, the way that within a grown man one often perceives the smile, the laugh, the stance that was his as a child.

But the child is no longer.

I close the door on the past for the final time. I know suddenly that it doesn't live within the walls of the house where I grew up. I know suddenly that it lives within me.

"I don't have to go to Randolph to go home anymore," I tell my son. I know finally that home is not just a building. It is a feeling, induced, nurtured, sustained by memories. "Anywhere I am is home," I explain.

My son just sighs, too young to understand.

Winter

Hanging On In Winter

Since October, I have been watching two leaves. At first I studied them from a sense of curiosity, wondering how long they would last. I saw them beaten by rain and whipped by wind. Still they clung, through October and November, huddled together, orphans of summer, the only survivors left on one branch of an oak tree in my front yard. By December, what had been curiosity had changed to awe.

They were a pitiful pair, brown and tattered like flimsy paper bags hidden under Coke cans and candy wrappers, occupants of any busy street. Every morning, I would come into my office and look out the window, sure that they wouldn't still be there, certain that the wind and the evening had finally defeated their tenacious hold and pulled them to their destiny.

But each morning there they were, more shrivelled, more vulnerable, yet still holding on.

One day, a week before Christmas, I watched them for a long time. It was a stormy day and the wind was brutal, shaking the house, whipping through the storm windows, sending slivers of cold air through caulking and cracks. This would be the day they fell. I knew it. I was certain. The wind keened, a high, terrifying squeal that grew stronger by the hour. Huge rubber barrels bounded down the driveway; a glass lantern, hanging next to the tree, shattered; Christmas wreaths strung from the windows plummeted to the ground.

I stared at those leaves, as brittle and as worn as parchment, and waited for them to be pulled away. But they endured. They stood straight, symmetrical almost, acrobats on a high wire, performing in unison, swirling, waving, shouting, "See me? I'm defying nature." Twins on a tightrope, the Great Wallendas, cavorting between hotels, daring the wind and gravity and their own belated fate.

All morning I kept stealing glances out the window, anticipating the fall, not wanting to miss it, though I'm not sure why. The wind wrestled the leaves for hours. Then it paused, and the sun emerged, a spotlight turned on in Heaven, and the sky changed from slate to Crayola blue.

A while later, the sun again burrowed behind dark, ominous clouds and the wind, sensing a final opportunity, turned rabid. The leaves no longer danced. They simply clung, thrashing against the tree. The rains came then, thick like foam, and the fight and the afternoon were long, too long. I turned off my office lights and left the room.

The next morning I looked out my window and smiled. The leaves were still on the tree. They had survived again.

Days passed. Christmas came and occupied my time. Then New Year's. Still, each morning when I opened my office door, I would glance out the window expecting an empty branch; but inevitably, the leaves were there, smaller, more crumpled, but surviving.

Maybe I got used to their endurance. Maybe I began to believe that they would thwart nature. They had overcome wind and rain and snow, all of the fall and some of the winter. I began to think they would hang from that tree forever.

It was a game, I know. The leaves were a metaphor. Something may appear to be weak and frail but is, in fact, strong and stubborn. The hour may be near, but not as near as we think. Nothing is certain, not even death. If I stand guard, nothing will happen. It was all a silly game.

One morning I noticed the leaves were gone.

I was at the front door with my daughter waiting for the school bus when I looked for the first time in a week, maybe two, at the familiar spot. I had been preoccupied. The shade had been down, the curtain closed. I forgot. I stopped noticing.

Now they are gone, two dead leaves, taken somewhere when I wasn't watching. It was their destiny to go. It was not mine to witness their leaving. The whole thing really doesn't matter.

But I feel strangely disappointed that I don't know how long they've been gone. That I didn't notice. For I had been watching. I did anticipate. But I became so used to the struggle, to the constant victories, that though in December I was awed, by January I took them for granted.

Just two insignificant leaves, I know. But a reminder: Pay attention. Keep watch. Nothing is forever. Not you, not me, not our children's childhood or our parents' old age. We can stand and wait and watch and anticipate, memorizing moments, preparing for events, but when we're not looking, when we're suddenly distracted, things change.

When It's Over

He watches her.

He sneaks peeks at her, pretending to be glancing in her direction, pretending to be interested in the person behind her, believing that if he avoids her eyes, if he focuses on her hair or her lips, she won't notice, and it won't count.

He stands in the middle of a crowd of kids, laughing, smiling, seemingly engrossed in what they're saying. But he isn't. His eyes are pulled to her, like pieces of iron in her magnetic field, and though he keeps looking away, though he keeps trying to get involved in the "So he goes" and "Then she says" — though he needs to be part of the crowd — his eyes won't let him.

He sees her smile at a boy next to her.

He sees her touch his arm the way she used to touch his.

He sees her lean toward him and laugh — he can't hear the laugh except in his mind, where it plays over and over, along with "I love you" and "There'll never be anyone but you."

He can't stop watching her though he tries. He can't stop watching because he loves her, the way she used to love him.

She used to stand next to him at the beach, at the Dairy Queen, in line at the movies, and gaze at him with such naked love and trust and yearning that he'd see adults look at him with — what was it — envy, longing, understanding? He didn't know. He didn't care. He only knew that with her he felt older, somehow. More important. In control.

"I've never felt this way before," she whispered to him when they were alone. "I've never loved anyone the way I love you." And the words, the kisses, the feelings were right out of a movie.

"You know what I love about him?" she confided to her friends. "We're so much alike. We like the same movies. We like the same music. We laugh at the same jokes. And he listens to me. He cares about how I feel. I've never met anyone like him."

She was so sure, so steadfast in her love. For months, every sentence included his name. She wore his ring, and he wore hers. She sent him cards, and he sent her flowers. At school, between classes, they would meet for two minutes, and the minutes sustained them through biology and history and Latin.

She wrote his name all over the margin of her notebook, and he called her every afternoon the second he got home.

She told him she liked the way his hair curled in the front, and the way he said, "I'll be waitin' on you," instead of "waiting for you." And he told her she was pretty, so pretty she didn't even need makeup.

Then something changed.

The first time she thought, "I wish he'd stand up straight. I wish he wouldn't act so wimpy around my parents," she felt awful. She denied the thoughts. She looked beyond the slouched shoulders at his caring eyes. She smiled at him. She took his hand. This is the boy I love! Will always love. Forever.

But increasingly little things started to bother her. The way he laughed after everything he said, an unnecessary hiccuping chortle. Had he always done this? Why hadn't she noticed?

The way he had of singing songs just a little ahead of the music so everyone would know he knew the words; the way he kept saying, "It's like" and "you know"; the way he always mumbled, "Yeah, I see what you mean," when he couldn't possibly see what she meant.

But it was the hot dog that made her realize she couldn't stand him another minute. She used to like the way he ate a hot dog — taking a bite from one end, then the other, then licking the relish and mustard off his fingers. How could she have put up with this? How could she have thought it was cute?

"Why can't you just eat it straight through?" she snapped one day in the middle of the fast-food restaurant. "I hate the way you do that!"

"I'm sorry," he said. And so was she. Terribly sorry.

"I don't love you any more," she finally told him, after weeks of pretending everything was all right, after being driven nearly crazy with his longing looks and his phone calls and his sighs. "But we can still be friends."

But we can still be friends. Six words guaranteed to break a heart.

"It's like a fairy tale in reverse," she told a friend. "All of a sudden my handsome prince turned into a revolting toad."

He didn't understand, of course. No one ever does. Two people fall in love at the same time, and it's everything they imagined, a long-playing love song they're sure will never end.

But then one of them falls out of love and the music stops, and the dance is over, and sometimes the stop is so abrupt, so unexpected that a heart suffers whiplash — especially a tender, young heart.

It's not a fatal injury, of course, only a common one. Still, it hurts just the same. Because he still loves her. He still looks at her.

And she doesn't even notice.

My Grandmother

There were times I thought she would live forever, the hard, crusty old woman who was my grandmother. Each September as the fragments of a family split apart by distance, careers, old hostilities and new resentments joined to add another candle to her birthday cake, we marveled at her resiliency.

My grandmother was not a kind woman. Her tongue was quick and sharp, her memories bitter, her perception of the world jaded by a past more real than the present.

She had four children, yet chose to isolate herself in a tenement in Cambridge, preferring Campbell's chicken soup to home-cooked meals at her daughter's. She lived for 86 years on an earth teeming with people, yet she detached herself, a solitary figure wasting away unnoticed; her death, like her life, uneventful.

Still, I can't help but wonder about the young Viola, the Viola with dark, wavy hair and expectation in her eyes who stares at me from an old tintype. Once she had been young and pretty, eager for all that life promised.

What dreams had she entertained? Had she wanted to change the world?

She married young and bore four children. There must have been happy moments. But her husband finally left her one night, after years of strained silences and midnight confrontations. What went wrong? What happened? The explanations we heard, the stories, were never the same. Only the bitterness remained constant throughout the years.

Until she was 75 she waitressed in a local tavern. A heavy-set woman with eyes of blue crystal, she played mother confessor to men whose tongues were loosened by too much Jameson's and a heightened sense of camaraderie. She seemed happiest then, almost cheerful in her role of counselor, psychologist and arbiter.

I remember visiting her one summer afternoon. I was a small child in a pinafore and black patent leather shoes sitting in the cool, darkened bar room sipping ginger ale. My grandmother was laughing and joking. I had never heard her laugh before and sat mesmerized, wondering what wonderful things these strangers were saying to make her smile.

Each night after work she would walk the half-mile back to her apartment, a woman alone at two in the morning. She was dauntless. Others stayed huddled behind locked doors at night, terrorized by the Boston Strangler who was roaming the city then, stalking victims. But she defied the danger.

After she retired, my grandmother became a recluse. She never went to a movie, the park, the corner store. She would not visit her daughters, even for the weddings, First Communions, celebrations, births and deaths that continued despite her refusal to witness them. One daughter shopped for her, cashed her checks and acted as her liaison with the world for 10 years.

And yet when my grandmother fell down her hard, wooden steps while getting the mail, she took herself to the hospital to have her broken arm set. "I didn't want to bother you," she told her daughter.

Feisty, spirited, independent, she had no need for human contact and could not accept human love.

And yet I wonder.

She always gave me Easter bunnies and teddy bears with soft fur and Muppet eyes that my mother claimed were useless but I adored.

When I'd visit, she'd tuck a dollar in my hand. "Buy yourself an ice cream," she'd order gruffly, avoiding my eyes, declining my kiss. Years later she'd do the same for my children. She never forgot a birthday or a holiday, her cards arriving dependably, crisp new dollar bills folded neatly inside.

We knew she was dying. Cancer ate away at her sturdy body, forcing her to compromise, to accept help. But only after a long, painful fight.

At home, bedridden, she stayed alone in a tenement that was an invitation to fire and derelicts. "Come live with us," her daughter begged. "You shouldn't be here by yourself. We love you. We want to take care of you."

But she lay in her makeshift hospital bed, hugging resentment, shouting at those who came to help.

She loathed her illness, and her irascible nature was augmented by her dependency. "Don't do it that way, do it MY way! The food's too salty. The tea's too weak. CAN'T YOU DO ANYTHING RIGHT?"

Eventually she was forced to go to the hospital and soon the disease ate away even her anger.

I wonder where she is now; if she's found the happiness that eluded her in life or if she is still encumbered by the resentments she carried about like pounds of extra flesh.

She was an unpleasant woman, but she was my grandmother, a kind of institution; not a charitable one, but a landmark nonetheless.

She was the hard, unyielding rock upon which our family was built. She chose to remain an island, isolated, cut off from the continent that was her family. She had little to do with us and by virtue of reason we should not feel her absence. Yet somehow the world today seems a bit emptier, the air thinner, the past more distant for her not being here.

Memories of Christmas

Here I am with my daughter, in Boston, walking along Tremont Street, the wind icy cold, so strong on our backs that it seems to be pushing us along, seems to be saying, "Hurry, or you'll miss something. Move quickly or that something will be gone."

"When I was your age I walked along this same street with my mother," I say.

"Did you come to Boston often, Mommy?" my daughter asks, shivering.

Not often. Twice a year. Once to go school shopping and again at Christmas, every Christmas, to stand in front of the windows of Filene's and Jordan's, then to see the "real" Santa Claus at Jordan Marsh.

"There weren't any shopping malls then," I say. "If you wanted to see Santa you had to come to Boston."

It has been a long time since this daughter and I have come to town for the holiday. Years before, when her brother and sister were small, I would make the trek because there was reason to then. The Enchanted Village at Jordan Marsh, the wonderful maze of animated Christmas characters and Christmas scenes now split up and sold to individual malls across the state, like the rides at Revere and Paragon Park, were part of every child's Christmas.

Now these landmarks are gone — as are all the landmarks of my youth. Strangers live in the house in which I grew up; the woods where I played have been bulldozed and paved, the library burned down, the old movie theater closed, so I don't anticipate memory on this trip. I don't expect to walk along the changed streets with the changed store fronts and remember how I felt three long decades ago.

And yet from the second we step out of the car onto the street there is this feeling, borne by the wind, accentuated by the fresh, cold air, that makes me hurry before the feeling is gone, that fills me with a litany of sentences all of which begin with "When I was your age."

My daughter and I stand in front of the windows of Jordan Marsh and I say, "When I was your age, they had the same musical bears only not just at Jordan Marsh but at Filene's, too. ALL the windows were for children back then."

In front of Filene's, we listen to a brass band playing Christmas carols and shoppers stopping to sing "Silent Night," and I say, "When I was your age, the Salvation Army people used to sing on ALL the street corners."

In Jordan's, in what used to be called Toyland, I look at the paltry display and say, "When I was your age, this whole floor was filled with wind-up animals and train sets and shelves of dolls, and it was the most wonderful place in the world."

In Filene's, where we go to browse, I am about to begin another sentence with "When I was your age," when the smell of the perfumes and the placement of the cosmetic department in the exact place it was 30 years ago makes me *become* her age. I am my daughter and my mother is me, the memory a piece of forgotten life found on some cutting room floor.

I have on my gray wool coat trimmed in black velvet, and a matching hat whose tie itches my neck; I have just come from seeing Santa, my for-a-girl present stuck under my arm.

I want to go home, but my mother lingers at some cosmetic counter. "You have lovely hands," the sales lady tells her. "You should take better care of your nails."

The sales lady is pretty, with dark hair and powdered skin and red lips; and nice, because she says to me, "Why don't you sit over here while I talk to your mother." She rubs cream on my mother's hands and files her nails and applies a coat of clear polish while I sit in my itchy coat and hat impatient to leave.

"You are a beautiful woman," she tells my mother and I stare at my mother's shiny, scrubbed face looking for what the sales lady sees.

She puts blush on my mother's cheeks and darkens my mother's lashes and fixes my mother's hair and in a while she is so transformed that even I, a child of 11, can see the beauty the sales lady has seen all along.

The kit my mother could buy to make herself beautiful is full of charcoals and reds and pinks. "Buy it, Mama," I say, "buy it so Daddy can see how pretty you are."

But my mother says no and buys a small bottle of clear nail polish instead.

I know why now, of course. But then I didn't know. And until today, right now, I didn't even remember the moment.

I look at my daughter and wonder how much she will remember, whether on a distant day when she is with her daughter, beginning her every sentence with "When I was your age," a fragrance, a song, even a simple trip to Boston will bring back the memory of today, this Christmas, and me.

Christmas Lights

"I wish the Christmas lights could be up all year long," I say to my daughter as we're driving home from gymnastics. In every house, candles light the windows and wreaths hang on the doors and even the humblest looks beautiful in the season's brilliant glow.

"It wouldn't be special if they were up all year," my wise 10-year-old says. "After a while you wouldn't even notice them."

I suppose she's right. I suppose the novelty is part of the joy. Driving down what is usually an unremarkable street and coming to a house bejeweled for the holiday, I am always a little awed and a lot impressed that someone took the time, made the effort to string lights around trees, spent days working at something that doesn't last, that's only temporary.

"It's like the forsythia, Mom. You know how every spring you say you wish the forsythia would stay yellow all summer long. Well, if it did, after a while you'd stop appreciating it. It would become just another tree."

She's the one who puts me in mind of flowers and gardens, this child who still sees the world through open, unassuming eyes. She's the one who makes me think about gardens and gardeners, how you have to admire people who take a piece of dirt and work it and feed it, weeding and watering, tending until there's a spot where beautiful living things grow.

I watch them in the spring, in the summer and the fall, the people who love the land, every day out in their yards, if only for an hour in the morning, pruning, planting all to make the world a lovelier place.

Now I watch the winter gardeners layered in parkas and scarves, unraveling strands of lights, placing colored bulbs, electrical this time, carefully, creatively, around trees and lamp posts, around whole houses and garages to create what is nothing less than a Christmas garden full of color and light.

Pride is what motivates them both. Pride and a need to create beauty where there is none. An old-fashioned virtue, this pride, the kind that makes me remember my grandmother sweeping the sidewalk in front of her house, scrubbing the steps that led up to her flat. Neither the sidewalk nor the stairs was hers, but hers in that the world is all of ours and if we can't even take care of what's right in front of us, then we all lose because the world then becomes a shabbier place.

It's not a shabby place, now. That old-fashioned pride is everywhere, in every window where a candle burns, on every door where a wreath is hung.

"Let's not go right home," I say to my daughter. "Let's drive around for a while."

So we do. Up and down streets we've never been before, past houses where lights flicker and illuminated Santas guide illuminated sleighs, past windows where Christmas trees glow, grateful that it's Christmas and that the season's special gardens are again in full bloom.

A Lost Legacy

The rubbish truck is out front. It will pick up our trash, then lumber across the street to where Mr. D. used to live and take away a couple dozen Glad bags that block one end of his driveway. A man's whole life is wrapped up in plastic.

Mr. D. died a month ago. Yesterday, someone — a distant relative? — came to clean up. He lugged dozens of trash bags to the top of the driveway. I wanted to go over and look in those bags to see if I could find in death what I never found in life: some clue to who this man, my neighbor for 18 years, had been.

Fifty years separated us, a formidable number; but it was more than time that kept us from being friends. His manner imposed a distance that inhibited friendship. Though neighbors, we remained strangers.

When I was newly married, I watched him one morning, from my living room window. He was shoveling snow in a coat so huge it dwarfed him, making him look like an old elf just down from the North Pole. A striped stocking hat pushed his ears out like handles on a soup tureen. He took tentative sweeps at the snow, as if he were testing its weight and saving his strength for later. Because he was old, because the day was cold, because my baby was asleep and my driveway was already clean, I put on my coat and boots and walked over to help him.

We did his driveway together. It took a long time because the driveway is wide and circular and he had to keep ducking inside to check on his wife, an invalid, and I had to keep running across the street to listen for my son. When we finally finished, we were both wet and tired. I asked him to come for tea. I had made blueberry muffins that morning and thought he might enjoy something warm and homemade. But he declined, saying, "No, no, it's too much trouble." I insisted. He said he'd join me later, at 4 p.m.

I set the table with my best china, got out cloth napkins and brewed loose tea. Promptly at four, the doorbell rang. There he stood, a frail old man, decked out in plaid pants and a black topcoat, clutching his hat, his eyes hugging the floor.

"Come on in," I said, smiling.

"I'm afraid I won't be able to join you for tea," he announced, as if he'd been practicing the sentence for hours. I didn't ask why. Something in his eyes wouldn't allow it. So we stood there silently, the January wind coughing spittles of snow which flecked the living room rug.

"If you don't mind, maybe I could take some muffins home," he said, this time the words pieced together like words on a ransom note.

He stayed by the door, hat in hand, his rubbers making puddles on the hardwood floor, while I wrapped six muffins in aluminum foil. "Thank you," he said, leaving, bowing almost, hurrying back across the street, his watery footprints all that remained of him.

That was 16 years ago.

Winters after that, he hired a plow to shovel his driveway. Maybe he was embarrassed by my help, or maybe he realized suddenly that he was 70, not 17. Afterwards, when we passed each other on the street, when he was walking his dog, or coming from the post office, our conversations were always bland. "How are you?"

"Fine, thanks. What's new?"

"Not much. Take care now."

About five years ago, his wife died. A few cars with out-of-state plates filled his driveway for a few days. Then the house was empty again. He had no children, no immediate family. Except for his dog, an ugly gray thing with yellow

eyes, he was alone.

He spent a lot of time with that dog. He walked him constantly, up and down the street, all times of the day and night. After the dog died, Mr. D. didn't walk anymore. He stayed in his house almost every day. The roses bloomed and he didn't prune them. The grass grew tall and he hired someone to cut it. In the fall, he got some boys to rake leaves.

In December, I invited him to Christmas dinner. "What time do you want me?" he asked, through his storm door. I said he was welcome any time but he pressed for a specific hour. "Well, why don't you come at noon?" I said.

Exactly at noon, the doorbell rang. There he stood, head bowed, stooped, an old tree that had weathered too many winters. He sat in the green chair in the living room all day. You couldn't tell what he was thinking. Not then, not ever. He had one expression that he wore all the time: the face a Fuller Brush man puts on when he's come to a house where the curtains are drawn and the grass is ragged and he doesn't know whether to walk up to the front door, or keep heading down the road but decides, what the hell, and, with great resolve, opens the gate.

We gave him a pen with a digital watch on the top — nothing big, less than five dollars at a drugstore. But his eyes shimmered and for a minute I thought he might cry. He stayed until seven that evening. He drank egg nog and ate turkey and took home half a mincemeat pie.

No one knows how long he was on the kitchen floor before the police found him. He'd had a stroke so he couldn't tell anyone. The doctors didn't think he'd survive. But he did. He went to a nursing home and in a few months was feeding himself. But then his leg got infected and antibiotics didn't help and the leg was amputated. After that, he deteriorated quickly. He died without ever coming home again.

Now he is gone and nothing remains of him. I walk outside and watch the rubbish men fill the truck with his things. It takes three of them five minutes. All the bags are neatly tied. Nothing spills to the street. I want to shout, "Stop!" to peek into even one bag, but of course I don't. I never peeked into his heart when he was alive.

I stand and watch the truck devour the bags and my heart aches. There should be more. More than trash bags and a slab of cement for a life that spanned nearly a century. It seems such a waste.

Uncle Shorty

Uncle Shorty was born in an elevator at the Quality Inn, Pentagon City, Washington D.C., sometime in January of '74. It was dinnertime and my children, then ages five and three, were moaning about having to use booster seats, those mini-chairs designed so that little people can see what they're eating — not an especially good idea considering children won't eat anything that doesn't resemble a Happy Meal.

"Booster chairs are for babies!" my five-year-old insisted. "SHE needs the chair," he said, pointing at his sister.

"I am not a baby!" the offended three-year-old wailed.

Then Uncle Shorty arrived and the question of who was a baby and who wasn't lost its importance. He came to life like Frosty. Words were his hat of magic, and he entertained the children that night and for at least a thousand nights thereafter.

"Uncle Shorty used to sit in booster chairs," I said, holding two little hands, walking into the restaurant. "When he went to college, a few people made fun of him. But they didn't laugh for long."

"He had to sit in a booster chair when he was in college?" my son asked. "Who is he, anyway?"

"Well, his real name is Amando Veluci III, but no one calls him that. They call him Shorty. I call him Uncle Shorty because that's what your grandfather told me to call him. He's the second cousin of a guy grandpa met during the war. Anyway, Uncle Shorty has this thing that looks like an umbrella but is really a folding ladder. He calls it a lumbrella and he carries it all the time because without it he can't even reach elevator buttons."

"He's that short?" the two of them chimed.

"Yes, he's very short," I said. "But very distinguished looking, too, what with his lumbrella and his three piece suits.

He has them made in South Africa. He used to live there when he was little."

A waitress carrying two booster chairs appeared. "I remember the time he came to visit you in the hospital right after you were born," I told my son who climbed into the seat without complaint. "He carried his lumbrella right up to the nursery window, climbed up, looked in and declared that you were the best looking baby in the nursery."

My son gave his sister a see, everyone-likes-me-better-than-you look. "But Shorty shouldn't have said that because there was this big guy standing next to him and I mean big, big as a giant practically, and he said to Shorty, 'Oh yeah! You think that scrawny kid back there's good lookin'? We'll you ain't seen my kid yet.' And the man pointed to a baby wrapped in blue right next to you. 'He's all right,' Uncle Shorty said, 'But I prefer the little fellow there.'

"Well right then that giant got so mad he kicked the ladder right out from Uncle Shorty and Shorty went flying. Banged his chin, bruised his elbow and hurt his pride. And the big guy just laughed, you know. A real bully."

Both children gasped. "Did he cry, Mommy?" they asked.

"He probably wanted to do," I said. "But instead he got up and brushed himself off and looked like he was going to walk away. But one thing about Shorty, he's not afraid to fight. He spent years getting his black belt."

"Did he hit him with it?" the littlest asked.

My son just sighed. "A black belt's when you're good at karate, dummy. You know? Like on Mighty Mouse."

I continued the story telling the children how Shorty defeated the brute with one punch in the nose.

"But how did he reach his nose?" they asked.

"He climbed right back up on his lumbrella, looked the

man in the eye, and aimed. Then he went back to gazing in the nursery window."

The children loved that story. All during dinner, they asked about Uncle Shorty. Where did he live? Did he have a job? Was he married? Would he come visit?

Uncle Shorty became part of our family that night and for years after there were few arguments about booster chairs. Or about going to bed early. Or about eating vegetables. "Uncle Shorty says that green beans made him strong."

Uncle Shorty loved to offer suggestions, to tell his point of view. And the children listened because he was *somebody*, he had been *somewhere*, he was the conqueror, the winner, the figure-it-outer. Shorty was short, but he was smart. You don't have to be tall to reach great heights, he often said.

Shorty, for the last five years, has been head of the elves. He got tired of traipsing around town with his lumbrella. His neck bothered him from having to look up all the time. Arthritis set in. So he headed north and wound up at Santa's Village where everyone, except Santa, is the same height. Shorty keeps in touch. He writes us letters and tells us what's going on. The last we heard, he was thinking about retiring.

I hope he doesn't. I hope he stays with Santa Claus and lives forever. People do, you know, up at the North Pole. It's a magical place. And Shorty belongs there, making toys, being a role model for the elves. Everyone needs a role model and everyone needs a little more magic. Uncle Shorty is both. May he live forever.

A Letter from Santa Claus

December 25

Dear World:

I understand you don't believe in me. I am a figment of the imagination, you say, a charade inflicted upon innocent children. I corrupt youth and inspire greed. You think I am a farce.

Ah, but you're wrong. I am neither a figment nor a farce. I am as real as you. In fact, I am you.

I'm the teacher who came to your house to help your son with the algebra he didn't understand, the friend who didn't desert you when illness struck, the woman who adopted the children no one else wanted.

I'm the stranger who held your baby the other day when it was pouring and your car was parked at the end of the mall. I'm the guy in the leather jacket who took the time to show you how to pump gas even though I was late for a date. I'm the sales clerk who wasn't rude when you returned a dress without the tags on a Friday night.

I'm the school bus driver who took care of your small daughter the afternoon you weren't home; the woman who visits your mother the days you are too busy. I'm every Boy Scout and Girl Scout leader, every Shriner, every coach, every religious teacher, every volunteer you ever met.

Sometimes, I am the absence of evil instead of the presence of good. I'm the fellow who doesn't pull into the parking space you've been guarding; the lady at the delicatessen who admits that you were in line first; the man who holds the door instead of holding you up; the teenager who doesn't steal your car. I'm the mother-in-law who doesn't carp, the guy who didn't break your heart, the girl who never stood you up, the child who always brought you joy.

I understand that it's easy for you to overlook me. Usually, I don't care. But at this time of year, when I hear people muttering about how there is no Christmas spirit, no true charity and no Santa Claus, I have to protest.

Just stop a minute and look around. I am everywhere. Those men and women standing on the corner ringing bells? Who do you think they are? The girls taping garlands on hospital walls? The children singing carols? The men delivering toys? The people cooking meals? The Elks, the Lions, the Knights of Columbus, every organization that has ever helped anyone?

I am all the fathers who have strung Christmas lights and spun tales to the delight of a child; every mother who's stretched cookie dough and time, who's scavenged for extra hours to work, to shop, to cook and to look relaxed watching "Frosty the Snowman" for the zillionth time. And I am, of course, all the children who use their red construction paper for Christmas cards, and their allowance for presents.

No Santa Claus? Humbug! Not to believe in me is to lose something of yourself. I am not just the spirit of Christmas, I am the essence of life. I am every glad tiding and good feeling you've ever entertained. I am selflessness and devotion. I am what gives humanity hope.

You expect me to tap you on the shoulder, to let you know I'm here. You anticipate the perfect setting: a little snow on the roof, a roaring fire, a clear winter's night. The children all nestled and snug in their beds.

But if the children are grown and the night isn't clear and the snow doesn't fall, what then? Disappointment? Disillusionment? If I don't slide down your chimney, does that mean I don't exist?

Of course not.

I am you. I am your goodness and your kindness and your charity. I am the best of what you can be, the realization of all your potential.

To deny me is to deny yourself.

As always,
Santa Claus

When Cancer Strikes

This is what it's like when someone you love gets cancer: There's a scream inside so shrill, so long and unbroken, that sinew melts and bone snaps and the weight of your own body and the labor of your own breath seem too much to bear.

It isn't like being hit in the stomach. It is like having an 18-wheeler parked on your chest. It isn't like falling off the end of the world. It is like being abandoned in space, in a universe of sharp-clawed, nine-legged, screaming, writhing things.

You wait with the person you love for the doctor to come into the examining room and you pray he'll have good news, *please God, let him have good news*. You sit and you talk about where you'll go to celebrate. Then a nurse comes in instead of the doctor and your eyes meet hers and she looks away and you think, she knows; but you deny her knowing.

Finally the doctor comes. He walks through the door and picks up the chart and you *know* that if he had good news he would say right away, "The tumor was benign." But you kid yourself. You think, no, he's just being cautious. Doctors are like that. He's just making sure he has the right person.

And so you hold your breath and you pray harder than you've ever prayed, bargaining, begging. *Please God, let her be all right*. But the doctor says the word anyway, "malignant," and the long, silent scream begins.

When the doctor takes the person you love into his office for the first cancer talk you don't hear his words. You sit and you watch him behind his desk, see his lips move, observe his head nod; but he is a TV without sound. You want to turn the station. You want to turn him off. You want to run away.

But you can't. So you listen in the hope, in the belief, that he will say, "Don't worry. I got it all. You're cured. Go home and be happy."

But he says instead, "There are no small cases of cancer.

172

Cancer is serious, but it is not fatal. Cancer can be treated. Cancer can be cured. There are worse things."

You can't think of one worse thing. You try. Your mind runs through a dozen possibilities, but keeps coming back to this one agonizing reality, the way your tongue would probe for a newly missing tooth.

The doctor spends a long time talking, assuring, reassuring, explaining, soothing. You want him to keep talking. You don't believe that there is anything worse than this, but you are afraid suddenly of silence.

You are most afraid at night. The dark creeps in and so does fear and sucks whatever air, whatever strength is left in you. In the dark you weep; in the dark you plead; in the dark you challenge God to tell you why.

Inexplicably, the world goes on when someone you love has cancer. It continues exactly as it always has. You go to work, to the grocery store. You smile, you laugh; you see a movie, you listen to music. But it is as if your soul has been beaten, whipped so hard and bound so tightly that it has shriveled and almost disappeared.

For the first month the cancer consumes you, too. You don't forget about it for a second. It is with you all day, all night. It is in your dreams and clings to you when you wake up screaming. Then one day it hides for a while. You read the newspaper and you realize you've been concentrating; you watch a basketball game and for minutes you forget.

The forgetting makes you sad, guilty, because the person you love isn't able to forget. You wish more than anything you could share her constant realization, carry some of her pain so that she could forget, too. *Give this dose of chemo to me*, you want to say. *Let me take a little so you won't have to bear so much. Let me lose a little weight; let me lose some hair.* A burden shared is a burden eased. Together, the intolerable can be tolerable.

But it doesn't work that way. You can sit right beside the person you love. You can hold her hand, read her mind, feel her fear; you can say, "Pass the cup to me." But the cup cannot be shared. You can love her, but you can't take the treatment for her. You can be right next to her, but you can't *be* her.

When the person you love has cancer, you rage, you question, you cry. The rage wanes, the questions get answered and the tears eventually stop.

What doesn't is the love. The love never stops at all.

Suddenly, The Memory Wins

When everyone is gone and the phone stops ringing and I have read all the notes, all the cards, all the kind condolences and have wrapped them in tissue and placed them in a box, and there is work to be done, a story to be written, and I am alone and have time to write it, I turn on the stereo instead and clean out the spice cabinet, full of expired medicines and empty salt shakers and old tins of sage and paprika.

And when the kitchen counter is littered with this stuff, not a speck of formica to be seen, I decide to do something else, to make beef stew and banana bread because it is damp and cold and beef stew would be good for everyone, solid, comforting food. I have three black bananas so I should put them to use, not throw them away, shouldn't I?

As the microwave defrosts the beef, I fry onions and listen to a song which, right in the middle, I suddenly cannot stand. So I leave the onions to search through the record cabinet for a softer tune, unable to believe that all these albums are really mine. When did I buy them? Why did I buy them? I forget all about the onions until the smoke alarm rings and in my effort to grab the smoking pan and prevent a fire, I knock to the floor a full bottle of Robitussin that instantly shatters.

I shut off the stove, wipe up the mess, dump the bananas in the trash, turn off the stereo, and walk out of the kitchen. What am I doing in there anyway? I don't like to cook.

What I *like* to do is be alone and sit in my office and turn on the computer and think and write and watch words become sentences, become thoughts I didn't even know I had, the process always intriguing and consuming.

Except for now. Now nothing intrigues or consumes. The phone rings and though I think I want to talk, I don't, so I end the conversation quickly. Though I think I want to write out my feelings, I do not. It is too soon for introspection. I want to keep memory at a distance, in sight, but not in hand. Later, I will think. Later, I will need to remember.

"Don't forget the caraway seeds," my mother used to say when I'd tell her that I was going to make her favorite bread. "A quarter of a cup, remember. It's better with a lot of caraway seeds."

The recipe called for a tablespoon, but my mother called for a quarter of a cup, so a quarter of a cup it always was. Cleaning out the spice cabinet, I came across caraway seeds, and then I remembered. And in that surge of memory, a surge that felt like electricity coursing through a cord that is hot and frayed and accidentally touched, there was raw pain and the fresh realization that I would never again make her an Irish bread because I would never again see her. I wasn't ready for the realization. I wasn't prepared.

A friend says that's what happens, that you expect holidays and birthdays and family occasions to be difficult after someone dies, and you steel yourself for them, as you would for a threatening storm. But that unexpected incidents are like accidents for which you cannot prepare. Simple things, as ordinary as finding a box of unopened caraway seeds and remembering for whom they were bought.

Time For Grandma

e don't visit her enough. Grandma — my children's, not mine, though I call her Grandma too — lives just two miles away, but two miles may as well be 100 most days. The world demands that we hurry, finish, achieve, perform, go to the store, get gas for the car, drop off the cleaning, drive here, drive there, cook, clean, work, run, race to fit it all in.

Grandma doesn't demand. She opens her front door and suggests that we come in and sit for a while, put our feet up, relax, slow down. We try. But seldom do we arrive as a family, all of us free at the same time. Instead we stagger into Grandma's like Pony Express riders, hostages of timetables that divide and subdivide our days and our lives into rigid blocks of time.

"I can only stay a few minutes," my daughter might say as she rushes in for a quick hello. "I just came to see how you're doing Grandma," my son will say, kissing her cheek. And instead of an "I wish you could stay longer. I wish you weren't always in a hurry," Grandma will smile and say "I'm glad you could come."

That's the way she is, a storybook grandma, white hair, soft lap, a candy jar full of M&M's, an understanding nature and constant, unconditional love.

When I was young, there were times I resented this woman. "Do you really think you should put the cradle right by the window?" she asked the day I brought my son home from the hospital. The window was sealed, I assured her. He'll be just fine there.

Fine? Fine! I can't believe she didn't insist. I can't believe she didn't say, "What are you nuts? You positively cannot put that baby there." But she was kind. She let me make my own mistakes. "Here, let me get a burp out of him," she would say when I couldn't, when all my pounding and pleading amounted to nothing. She would take my son from my arms and no sooner was he in hers than he would let out a huge, happy burp.

I think he always knew how much she loved him. I think he always sensed his importance in her life. She would stop ironing, stop cleaning, stop whatever she was doing simply to sit with him in her lap, rocking him and singing the Scottish songs her mother had sung to her. And I, in my youth, would look at this woman with my son in her arms and feel a kind of envy that she was loving someone I thought belonged to me.

What a fool I was. I don't remember when I grew up, when I came to appreciate her love, when the wonder of it occurred to me. All I know is that for years I have depended upon it.

During a recent heat wave, when the air sapped ambition and energy, my daughters and I fled to Grandma's. It's a thing we haven't done since winter, just sit around Grandma's house, drinking tea, eating cookies, talking.

Grandma doesn't have the typical trunk full of old shoes and dresses for us to explore. But she has a head full of memories which, when we beg, when we have time, she shares with us.

We had time then, so she told us again, because we never grow tired of hearing about growing up in Scotland, about heating water in the fireplace and taking baths in a tub in front of it ("In front of your whole family, Grandma?"). About walking to school every day, and stopping at the butcher's, about the happiness she felt when her father finally came home from the war and her grief a year later when he died and left her, this time forever.

Always when she talks about the past, Grandma transforms a little. In the middle of a story when she is describing a dress she wore, or a place where she went dancing, we can see a bit of the girl she was. Her eyes flash and her words skip like a schoolgirl's telling a tale, and she grows young before us as she recalls her youth, her friends, and Ian, a boy she knew in Scotland who, when he grew up, sailed to America solely to see her.

The story of Ian is our favorite, a love story of the most romantic kind. Ian arrived unannounced after a separation of 10 years, knocking on her door on a Wednesday. But she had a date with the man she would marry and didn't see Ian until Friday night when they went dancing. They stayed out late, hitting all the popular New York night spots — The Cotton Club, The Astor Roof, The Taft Grill — and on Saturday, wearing her best suit and purple pillbox, she went with him to the 1938 World's Fair. Ian bought her roses, took her to dinner at the Astor Hotel, and after dinner walked reluctantly with her back to his ship where she told him goodbye.

"I was in love with someone else," she explains simply when we ask her why.

Mostly we think of Grandma as "Grandma," a woman who was born with gray hair and kind eyes. The heat wave slowed us down and allowed us time to see, that before there was a Grandma named Peggy Beckham, there was a young woman named Peggy Duff.

The Shades of Winter

t's 7:30 in the morning and the kids are about to leave for school.

"Come here for a second and look out the window. What color are those pine needles in the garden?" I ask.

"They're rust," my 11-year-old says.

"They're brown," my 17-year-old contradicts.

"They look orange to me," a neighbor's child adds.

For days I have been looking at those needles trying to figure out exactly what color they are. Every morning, when the sun is behind them, they have a pinkish hue and appear translucent, more like a shimmery vision than real pine needles covering the ground. But when there isn't any sun, when the day is gun-metal gray, they look flat and dull and uninspiring.

Until you get up close. Up close, even on the dullest of days, the pine needles and the oak leaves trapped by the fence and the squat shrubs a few feet away and the gangly trees in the background, looking as thin and brittle as pencils, don't look uninspiring at all.

Up close — that's the key. Most winters I stay in my house, heat turned up, long underwear on, counting the days until spring. Most winters I'm so busy wishing for green grass and flowers that I don't give winter a chance.

But this has been a mild winter, the days so warm that even the crocuses are confused, dozens of them already searching for the sun. Like them I have searched, too, setting out for walks down streets that seem foreign, so unfamiliar are they in their clarity and sharpness. I am used to a world in bloom, a world softened by filtered light and rounded trees. I am used to a dressed-up, fancier place.

Stripped of its brilliant colors, without the fullness of leaves and the fragrance of flowers, without a warm yellow

sun as a spotlight, I expected the world, up close, to be nothing but bare bones. It looks skeletal from behind closed windows.

But walking, I have discovered that I like the world unadorned. I like its keen shapes and its sharp angles, the way each branch on each tree looks as if it has been outlined with a fine-tipped fountain pen.

Sometimes, when thin clouds hide the sun, a milky iridescence covers the world, as sheer and sweet as mother's milk on the lips of a child. And sometimes, just before the sun sets, the browns and rusts and greens on the ground blend with this strange iridescence and combine with the blue of the sky, and the air becomes glazed with a hint of pink and blue and orange.

I imagine Adam walking around in his garden that first winter on earth trying to find words for the colors of winter grass and the hue of winter sky — Tan. Beige. Hazel. Umber. Maybe in the language Adam spoke these words were as beautiful as the images he was trying to convey. Maybe he thought for months before choosing one, the way parents try out dozens of sounds before choosing a baby's name.

I feel like Adam, new to this beauty, awed by it, transfixed, discovering winter for the first time.

The Silent Voice

He died last fall. The line at his wake stretched at least a half a mile. Afterward, for weeks, for months, people thought about him. But gradually they forgot. He had been a part of their lives, but he had not been their whole life. Only his mother continued to grieve.

His death aged her. She became creviced like the land that skaters walk on, their sharp, silver blades gutting into the earth as if it had no feelings. She became ridged and rutted. She was the earth. She was the soil in which her son had grown.

She functioned. She cooked. She talked. Sometimes she even smiled. But her eyes blazed with pain. So people, when they met her, avoided her eyes. They stared at a shirt collar that needed ironing, or at the sleeves of a jacket that hung below her hands or at a necklace that said "Number One Mother," a necklace that her fingers kept touching.

In the beginning her husband and daughter shared her sorrow. But her husband had work and her daughter had school. They moved on. They seemed to pass the loss, like determined game pieces moving toward a visible goal. Their eyes became misty when his name was brought up and her daughter would sometimes toss in the night and her husband would sigh, sitting in front of the television watching the Bruins. But they survived. In the evening they brushed their teeth and slipped into their beds and slept; and in the morning, they showered and kissed her goodbye, leaving her alone with her memories.

It was then, before the school buses lurched up the street, before the milkman rattled the front door to remind her to take in milk that spoiled in the refrigerator because he wasn't around to drink it anymore (but she couldn't bear to stop getting it, to acknowledge that he would never again sit at the kitchen table, never again drink an entire quart in a gulp) — it was then that the house was so still she could hear the blood flowing through her veins, feeding her heart. Then she would wonder why she continued to exist, why she had not died with him, as she had come alive when he was born.

For weeks after his death she went into his room and cleaned. She opened the windows and pushed up the screens so that leaves floated in, and a few stalwart bees. She should have smelled autumn in that room — the oak tree rustled and a distant chimney sputtered smoke and the light filtering in was Halloween orange — but she could smell only her son.

His fragrance was everywhere: in the curtains, in the rug, in each of his drawers. She stood in his room and cried. It wasn't fair. How could a smell survive when he didn't? How could his books still be on his desk, his football trophies positioned exactly as he had placed them? What was his sweater doing neatly folded when he was becoming dust in the ground? What good was it all when things remained and people didn't?

She opened his closet and touched the sleeve of his coat and felt his warmth as if he had just worn it, as if he were in the next room, as if she could hurry down the hall and touch him, too. She wrapped herself in his coat, inhaling the old suede and the new cologne he had just begun to wear, and the strong, male scent that was him.

She began wearing the coat around the house. "Why are you doing that, Mom?" her daughter asked. "It's just going to make you more upset."

Couldn't her daughter understand? The coat soothed her. Her son's arms protected her. He was her.

One morning she took all his baseball cards and spread them out on his bed. She picked up everyone, read it, touched it, then piled it according to teams. She separated the American League from the National League. She put pitchers first and catchers last. She made a separate pile for all-stars and cards that were odd-sized — cards he had found in boxes of Drake's Cakes or Hostess Twinkies. She put elastics around the piles and stored them in a shoe box. Then she sorted his socks, folding them and unfolding them until the light in the room grew dim and she remembered that she had to make dinner.

She read his school notebooks, studying the way he made his numbers, stunned that he crossed his sevens. How long had he made them that way? Why hadn't she noticed? She read "Of Mice and Men" because he'd read it. And she listened to the music on his cassettes, songs he'd taped from the radio, full of drums and cymbals and high, uneven notes.

One day she was listening to a tape he'd made and the notes were thin and reedy and she found herself not minding the music at all, liking it, in fact. She had the lights on in his room because the day was gray and bleak and she was sitting on his bed listening, leaning against his pillow, his jacket hugging her, when she heard his voice. "Hey, don't fool around with that thing. I'm taping a song with it."

She froze. His voice, clear and strident and so achingly alive was a reminder of all she had lost, all that was missing without him. She felt the blood drain from her face. She saw her hands shake. And she heard her heart heave deep in her chest, and sigh like a tire that is flat and has been forced to spin just a little longer and is able to spin no more.

She looked around, needing to see his lean frame in the doorway. But he didn't appear. And the empty space, full of shadows and possibility, defeated her.

Last Times

For each of my children, I kept a baby book. In them, I recorded all the firsts: first picture, first laugh, first tooth, first step, first word, first Christmas, first day of school.

I took note of these moments because I wanted to preserve my children's childhoods. I thought that firsts were a kind of yardstick, the best way to measure a child's growth.

But I was wrong. Growth is more subtle. I should have been on alert, not for the first times, but for the last times.

You see, a kind of psychic alarm rings at every first in our lives. Because of that mental commotion we attribute inflated significance to these firsts. It's understandable. We can't help but remember and romanticize the things for which we've longed: our first day of school, our first friend, our first kiss. These things stand out simply because they stand alone. They're like a solitary person in a waiting room. There's no way not to notice them.

Last times, like old friends, are overlooked. Last times are remembered, if they're remembered at all, by their absence, not by their presence.

I am considering this today because it is snowing, and snow and no school have always meant isolation from the world, marathon games of Monopoly, gallons of hot chocolate and dozens of chocolate chip cookies warm from the oven.

But not today. Today my children have chosen to be with friends — even the youngest — and I am left home, alone. I should be happy. I have time to write. But I'm sad.

You see, I've missed another last time. I was in the kitchen, stirring batter, listening to someone scream, "It's my turn to be the dog cuz' you were the dog the last time!" I was counting pink and yellow money when the cries stopped and the children disappeared and I was suddenly alone, unable to remember when they were all here. Was it a few weeks ago? Or was it last year?

When my son was small his grandmother gave him a black, wooden totem pole, which he put on top of his bureau. That position was fine for the day because in the light the totem pole looked like what it was: a carved piece of wood. But at night, the pole grew ominous. Eyes gleamed and mouths twitched and it seemed to breathe. So it was taken each evening from the room and placed in the hall facing the wall like a chastised child.

For months? For years? I walked past that totem pole on the way to bed. I couldn't help noticing it. It was always in my way. But it spent so many nights ostracized, it became such a fixture, that it grew invisible and I don't remember when it gave the corner back to the dust motes that cling there now.

The totem pole is no big deal. Except that maybe when it left the hall it marked the beginning of the end of one boy's childhood. A small thing, really, except when it's your boy. It was just one more last time that snuck away on cat's paws.

I suppose some last times are memorable. The last night at home sleeping in your own bed before you get married. The last time you see a friend before she moves, hugging her, promising to write. The last kiss goodbye at an airport. But these are recognizable last times. So you take note and remember.

But most last times are illusive. Their leaving is as imperceptible as spring's burgeoning to summer. One day the oaks are new green and the air is heavy with lilacs and it feels as if it will be spring forever, but when you look again, the leaves are moss green and the lilacs have died and though you've been there all along, inhaling the air, living in the shadow of the trees, you never notice.

Mommy! Mommy! Don't shut off the hall light. The monsters will get me! And the light shone all night, piercing the dark, reminding me by its presence that a child slept nearby. But the hall light has been dark how many years? I don't know. I don't remember.

Mommy, will you read me a story? And I wouldn't want to; the efforts would seem huge, "The Cat in the Hat" boring. But the hole that is left when no one begs for a story is big and the pity is I don't know when the story-reading stopped.

Mommy, will you zipper this? Can you get me a glass? I can't reach.

There is still the youngest. I watch her sleep with Teddy in her arms. She stumbles into my bed in the middle of the night. I am still — almost — her best friend.

But I am on alert for change: For the last time she'll climb on my lap just to tell me she loves me; for the last time she'll call from a friend's to say hello; for the last time she'll reach under her pillow, find a tooth replaced by a dollar and know beyond a doubt that the tooth fairy came.

There will be no warnings for these last times. No "Shoppers, the store will be closing in 15 minutes. Please take your purchases to checkout." Nothing. You do something every day for years and you think you will be doing it forever. But there is no forever. Everything has a last time.

Spring

Symphony of the Subway

It lasted a minute, perhaps two, an infinitesimal moment of a person's life. It was nothing but it was everything, solemn yet joyful, a moment full of beauty.

It floated across the tracks, a plaintive tune, a haunting combination of sharps and flats produced on a violin by a man in an overcoat and a beard.

At first I didn't see him. I just heard the notes, divine and pure, making me think of the orchestra at Auschwitz assuaging the doomed crowd.

This day's crowd was not doomed, only chilled and indifferent. They didn't walk, they shuffled. They looked, but didn't see, staring vacantly ahead waiting for the beast that would gobble them up only to spit them out at their several destinations.

But they didn't mind. They were used to being churned like butter. They were used to sitting cramped or standing crushed inside the creature's gloomy intestines.

They were used to anesthetizing themselves against the privations of subway travel, a mode of transportation relegated to underground because it could not endure the scrutiny of day. What they were not used to was the sudden intrusion of beauty into this scene.

Across the tracks, on the outbound side, a train thundered into the station, shrieking as if angry that someone had committed it to stop. The doors creaked open. The beast made its evictions and other passengers hurried to take their place.

Full again, it sighed, heaved its doors shut and lunged down the track, sounding like a dozen electric saws whining in disharmony.

And then the music came.

In the quiet between trains, this place with its urine-spattered walls, its Mazola scented air, its throngs of unblinking, stone-faced strangers all shut within themselves, became a concert hall, a grimy subway station hallowed by a man with a violin and a bow.

His music was magic. It made the cold, dirty concrete disappear. It made a businessman loosen his grip on his briefcase. It made an old woman dressed in black smile.

The notes, as thin as china and as clear as crystal, were haunting, joyful, sad, aching. The combination of all life, the culmination of all emotion. They penetrated layers of clothes, thick wool sweaters and down coats, hats and scarves and gloves, and seeped into tiny pores, feeding hearts and minds hungry for beauty.

Just seven sounds and a few variations, joined and disjoined, elongated and aborted, fashioned on a piece of wood with strings attached. And the message that poets have been trying to convey for centuries was airborne, drifting through the subway station, soothing and searing the souls of strangers who, from this day forth, would share one common memory.

How long did it last? What was the song the musician played? Does it matter? The moment could never be duplicated. It was the beginning of life, the summer's first rose. It was a glimpse of divinity, an intimation of pure joy.

So even as the beast approached, even as its eyes grew brighter, even as it wailed into the station and lurched to a stop — even then, when the notes from the violin were swallowed up and could be heard no more...

They could be heard forever.

Twenty Years — and Growing

Twenty years — 7,305 days — half my lifetime, married to the same man. "You're too young to get married," two sets of parents told us. "Finish college first. Work a year. Give yourselves time. Then you can get married. You have your whole lives ahead of you. Why are you in such a hurry to get tied down?"

Tied down? Marriage wouldn't tie us down. Marriage would give us the freedom to be together.

We drove around in his car listening to the Beach Boys on the radio, ("Wouldn't it be nice if we were married...") planning our lives. I wanted to cook for him. I wanted to iron his shirts and make his breakfast before he left for work in the morning and sit beside him late at night, an audience for his coughs and sighs.

"Wait," our parents begged. But we didn't. I was 20 and he was 21. "Wait" was not a word we wanted to hear.

When I look back at our wedding pictures I am struck by our youth, by our child-smooth faces. I stare at the photographs and remember how I felt then: old, so why were they telling us we were young? I know why now: they told us because we were.

And yet I would do it again — marry young. For in the beginning were some of the best times. Work, school, scrub the house, paint the baseboards, spackle the walls, "Want to have friends over?" Every night a party. "Care for some wine? How about cheese? Come back again." Seeing the envy in other couples' eyes when they left and went their separate ways and we said goodnight at our front door, side-by-side, together.

Sometimes I missed my mother. If I ached for anyone or anything, it was for her. My husband (I used to make up sentences just to say these words. "MY HUSBAND said this.

MY HUSBAND has one of those. Do you mind if I call MY HUSBAND?" the words like a prayer) traveled a lot and when he did, I would pack a bag and go home to my mother. "You're not going home," he would remind me every time. "This is your home now."

But it wasn't, not really. It was a make-believe house which I scrubbed and polished and cleaned and played in, exactly as I'd played in the old chicken coop my best friend, Rose, and I had scraped and scrubbed into a clubhouse. I loved that chicken coop for an entire summer between fifth and sixth grade, and I loved the house where I lived with MY HUSBAND, but home was where my mother was. Home was where I grew up. Where the bathtub felt familiar. Where I could go and have someone take care of me, not where I took care of someone.

In the beginning, I returned to that home often. Then my son was born and his grandparents preened and his father strutted. I swaggered too, and I dressed him up and took him places just to show him off, and didn't go "home" quite as often because after he was born, it seemed I was home, after all.

Looking through the picture albums, I can feel again all that old happiness and can hardly notice the change that forced the pair of us to grow up. The absence of my husband's father and my mother is not all that obvious. And yet in our lives their absence loomed. When my father-in-law died and my mother became ill, I couldn't envision the years ahead. But they happened. Here they are in living color. Life went on.

On the occasion of our 20th anniversary, I study those old pictures in search of the young people we were, amazed and proud that we lasted. We were too young, they all said. But our youth turned out to be an asset.

"Isn't it boring being married to the same man for 20

years?" my daughter asks, plopping herself down to look through the pictures with me.

The "same" man? These words are wrong. Even in the pictures you can see he isn't the same man, just as I'm not the same silly girl who thought ironing 100 percent cotton shirts the ultimate act of love. The boy I married didn't know how to make chicken piccata or entertain a child on a long trip, or do Cookie Monster and the Three Bears in Cookie Monster's voice.

The boy I married wasn't as understanding, as kind, as quick-witted or quick to forgive, and wasn't nearly as thoughtful. The boy I married couldn't hold a candle to the man I am married to today.

Real Music

When she first left, two, three years ago, I wrote about her. How dancing school wasn't the same without her there; how a tape recorder could never take the place of Elaine Richardson's piano playing.

For nine years I had walked up the steps to the trill of her tunes, opened the door to see little girls in different sizes, stretching, smiling, shuffle-ball-stepping, while Mrs. Richardson sat at the piano, pencil-straight, her fingers ballerinas on the keys.

Her music was the soundtrack of my children's lives. My older daughter was five when she began dancing school; my youngest felt the notes in the womb. When the music stopped, the place seemed pale. It wasn't the same. Of course, we were sad. Dancing had lost some of its magic.

But time has a way of making you forget, and I adjusted, the way I do in winter, to bare trees and cold, not remembering that trees really do blossom and summer air is always warm and sweet.

But yesterday the world bloomed again.

I was picking up my daughter and the day was gray and rainy, and I was a little gloomy, too. It was an effort to drive to the church where dancing classes are held because I had other things on my mind, other things to do, and was full of them when I opened the church door and ran right into a group of spirited notes that came bouncing down the steps.

They weren't *different* notes. They were the same set of tunes I hear every week because it is a tape of Mrs. Richardson's playing that has taken her place, that the children dance to again and again.

But these notes were alive, crisp and clean, as different from tape as real laughter is from the canned laughter you hear on TV. So before I opened the door to the class, before I saw

her poised at the keyboard, I knew Mrs. Richardson was there.

And it was a gift, August in April, something unexpected, wild flowers at the side of the road. I sat down and let the notes work their magic, remembering the years of this, recalling how every time I walked into this room, no matter how tired I was or preoccupied or sad, I would lose myself in the music, in the click of the taps, in something more than myself.

The children must have felt the difference, too, because they danced with vigor and joy, more enthusiastic than I'd seen them for a while, the notes inspiring, almost directing them.

Next week Mrs. Richardson won't be here. Her husband is ill and needs her at home. I'll walk up the steps, as I've done for the past two years and I'll hear the recording and I will feel hollow.

But after a while I'll forget. You live in the shadows long enough and you stop believing in the light. And it's all shadows. The images on TV. The voices booming from radios. Everything second-hand.

Except sometimes, briefly, like in a small dance studio in a small town where a lovely lady who makes magic with music can transform the ordinary into something special.

An Easter Tree's Magic

The first tree was for the children. They were asleep and I was awake, and the sun was shining. It was warm — unusually warm for Easter morning — and the world beckoned. I must have walked outside. I must have decorated the trees, for when my children awakened, the scraggly, half-dead peach tree in our back yard was dressed in lollipops, and M&M's and jelly beans covered the ground.

"Why, look!" I said to the sleepy towheads in Dr. Denton's. "Look at that tree. It's magic!"

And they climbed up to the window and gasped, "Daddy! Daddy! Come quick and see what the Easter Bunny did."

The tree was the highlight of that day. "You should have seen it, Grandma," my son exclaimed. "There were so many lollipops and jelly beans. I bet if I followed the trail I'd have found out where the Easter Bunny lives."

Those were golden days when my son and daughter wished upon every star, never doubting that their wish would come true; when they believed that there really was a pot of gold at the end of a rainbow; when they were certain that, in the middle of the night while they slept, teddy bears talked and Easter bunnies made special deliveries.

The next year an entire nursery school class had heard about the wonderful tree that would appear on Easter morning. "Do you suppose if we wrote a letter, the Easter Bunny would come early and we could have a party so everyone could see the magic?" my son asked.

"I don't see why not," I said.

So the bunny arrived a week ahead of time, and a dozen four-year-olds, dressed in snowsuits and mittens, scooped up candy from the frozen ground and begged to be lifted so they could reach the Tootsie Pops hanging from the branches.

The following year we moved and left the peach tree

behind. "But how will the Easter Bunny find us?" my son cried from his new room. "What if he thinks we still live there and he doesn't come here?"

"Don't worry," I said. "He'll know. I promise."

That Easter, the tree was a collection of forsythia and pussy willows stuck inside a huge vase, placed in the center of the family room. That was also the year Peeps and chocolate bunnies and Brighams' ice cream certificates were added to the lollipops, as compensation for the much-missed peach tree.

"This is the best tree ever!" the children exclaimed.

"This is the best tree ever," they shouted, year after year.

But too soon they grew up. Too soon they stopped shouting and stopped believing. Too soon the questions came: "How does a bunny get the money to shop at Brighams?" and "Why is his handwriting so much like Dad's?"

"You can't fool us," they said, older and wiser. And the tree, shorn of its purples and yellows and blues, stripped of its charm, wasn't magic anymore.

The next year, I couldn't bear not to have the tree. There was another child, a baby, who would someday believe, but I couldn't wait. I needed to believe then — not in the Easter bunny — but in the promise of spring. So I put up the tree for me.

I put it up weeks before Easter, filling a planter with forsythia, hanging wooden eggs from the pussy willows, filling in the bare spots with baby's breath. Without the candy, though, the tree was dull. I added daffodils and crocus, but it wasn't the same. It looked like a plant, not a tree.

So I brought silk flowers and wrapped them around the empty branches and the tree became beautiful. Every year I added more branches and more flowers until eventually, instead of putting the silk orchids and gardenias, the paper lilies and lilacs on bare limbs, I dug out our small artificial

Christmas tree and decorated it instead. Then I added stuffed bunnies and ceramic lambs, plastic Peeps and a family of tiny rabbits a friend made for me.

And so the tree evolved. This year it sits in the living room decorated with tiny white lights and bright flowers, surrounded by pink and green plastic grass, and my youngest's family of stuffed rabbits.

My older children, the ones who once bragged about their Easter tree, are embarrassed by its presence. But the youngest loves it. She invites friends over and they play with the bunnies and lambs and I listen to them talk. I hear my daughter explain how the tree is a tradition, how I decorate it now but how, a long time ago, the Easter Bunny taped lollipops and candy all over it.

"On Easter morning he always leaves a trail of candy from my room, down the stairs and out the door," she says. "Maybe if I follow it, I'll find out where he lives and I can ask him to put lollipops on the tree again. What do you think?" she asks her friend.

"I think it's a great idea," she says.

The tree is making magic again.

A Perfect Prom Night

I know that beauty is only skin deep. I know that it's what's on the inside that counts. On the inside, she has always been beautiful. But on the outside, though she has glowed and sparkled, she has never looked as lovely as she did last night.

She appeared at the top of the staircase like a vision, a Cinderella transformed. I had never seen my daughter with flowers in her hair. I had never seen her wearing a full length gown, except in play, except when she dressed in her grandmother's clothes and her grandmother's furs, pretending to be grown up.

Now, suddenly, she was grown up.

She didn't teeter on her heels. She didn't giggle as she walked. She didn't curtsey to some fantasy prince only she could see. She floated down the steps like a whisper, a princess from birth, all those years of pretending having culminated in this moment.

We chose her gown weeks ago and when she slipped it on in the store I caught a glimpse of how she would look the night of the prom. The royal blue taffeta matched her eyes and the dress's lines accentuated her small waist and when she walked, the dress swayed as if it were aching to dance.

But in the store, in the three-way mirror, despite the fact that this was a real gown for a real prom, she still appeared to be a little girl pretending. Her sneakers were in the corner and her jeans were on the floor and she was giggling, trying on half a dozen dresses just for fun, making faces in the mirror, prancing around in hats and veils, as if all of this were make believe.

Even as we shopped for accessories, for the perfect gloves and jewelry, for matching shoes and bag, it remained a game. She would go upstairs the night of the prom and fuss with her hair and her makeup, and slip on the beautiful gown and come downstairs, and look lovely, yes; but she would still be my little girl.

I think her transformation surprised even her. Maybe it was the dress. Maybe it was the way she curled her hair. Maybe it was the soft spring night, or the afternoon light, or the scent of lilacs, or the Mills Brothers singing "Queen of the Senior Prom" over and over again. Maybe it was none of these things or maybe it was all of these things. Maybe, it was just her fairy godmother, sneaking in an upstairs window, waving her magic wand, giving my daughter the night. Every girl's a princess at least one night in her life.

Her prince arrived, not on a white horse; princes don't ride white horses anymore. They rent limousines, instead. My daughter's prince emerged from his, looking as if he had his own fairy godmother, for he, too, appeared to have stepped right out of a story. He wore white tails and his cummerbund and tie matched her dress, and when he gazed at my daughter the look in his eyes matched the look that is in hers every time someone mentions his name.

I cried, of course, for the same reason I cried when I first held her, for the same reason all mothers cry. I cried in wonder at her being, and I cried in gratitude for her being mine.

Life isn't a fairy tale, I know. One night, no matter how perfect, can't last forever. Even Cinderella couldn't return to the ball.

But one night can be remembered forever, one perfect night, the night of the senior prom.

Teddy Grows Old

He was a fine looking bear when he was new, white and fluffy with shiny, brown eyes and a black felt nose and a white satin tie on which the words "I Love You" were embossed in red. He had satin ears then, too, but only on the inside, on the hearing part, spotted with polka dots to match his tie. In pictures, he looks cute and loveable, but in no way extraordinary.

I didn't have an inkling that he was special. He was a gift from my mother to my infant daughter, but one of many gifts, certainly not outstanding in any way. He wasn't a "Wow, look at the size of that bear," creature, a huge huggable hulk that takes up half a room. And he wasn't a musical bear, either. He didn't sing "Lullaby and Goodnight" or "Twinkle, Twinkle, Little Star," like some other bears did. He was quiet and unassuming and when I placed him in my daughter's crib next to a natty looking Paddington Bear dressed in a red felt hat, and a black bear who could sing three different tunes, I figured this little bear didn't stand a chance.

But it was this little bear for whom my daughter reached. I don't know when she began hugging him and him alone. It seems she always has. Even when she was tiny, even before she could sit up or say "Mama," there was Teddy, nestled in her arms. Maybe she chose him because he was small and fit so snugly under her chin. Or maybe she chose him because he was quiet and his eyes were kind and he wasn't so concerned with strutting his stuff — making sure his slicker was on straight, or singing in the right key. So he had time to listen to her.

And listen he did. He heard her first sounds, her first words, the murmurs and sighs of all her childhood nights. He was her steadfast friend, the one she reached for in the dark when she awoke; the one she reached for in the day when she was sad.

When she went to sleepovers, she put a doll's T-shirt on Teddy and dragged him along. When she went skiing, she got him a ski hat and he went skiing, too. On every vacation, Teddy always came along.

But age is catching up to Teddy. Age is taking its toll. You see, all the time my daughter was growing up, Teddy was growing up, too. But bears grow differently. They don't grow taller and bigger like children do. If they are loved, they actually shrink a little. Their fur gets matted down in the places where they are squeezed, and their ears, once straight and perky, sag from being hugged. And sometimes, when they are *really* loved, their felt noses wear off, too.

A bear's life span is also very different from a person's. A bear's life span is much shorter. Children grow into adults who live an average of 80 years. Bears, when they are lucky, live an average of 12 years, until the children who love them grow up.

Teddy is almost 13, an old, old man. His eyes, once so shiny, are completely gone and you can see only the stitching where his mouth was. The "I Love You" tie has been missing for years, his ears are frayed, and when he sits up, which he can do only with help, his head flops to one side. Even his color is bad. His white fur, what little that hasn't been loved off, is a dingy shade of gray.

But, oh, how this bear is still loved. Others continually try to replace him. A huge creature won at a carnival; a Felix from Filene's, a soft blonde bear compliments of Aunt Janet.

But Teddy reigns supreme. He may be old and worn and not as cuddly as he used to be. He may need some help sitting up; but he still fits under my daughter's chin and he's still the one she sleeps with every night.

He won't be around for always, I know. Even very loved bears don't last forever. But very loved bears are remembered forever, and memory at least is for always.

Digging Soil for the Soul

I don't know them. I don't know their names or their occupations. I don't know if they're young or old, rich or poor, single or married or divorced. I don't know what motivates them, why they put on work gloves in March and zipper-up their old jackets and head outdoors to clear away dead brush while I sit inside waiting for a sunnier, more cordial day.

I don't know what prods them into pruning and cleaning, dragging out the wheelbarrow and the trash bags, tending to the flower beds, cutting and fertilizing the lawn, making their plot of land look like something out of *House and Garden* while I look at the enormity of the task and procrastinate again and again.

I don't understand what inspires these people, what makes them so fastidious, but I admire their work and appreciate their effort because their efforts result in gardens that make the world a lovelier place.

My own flowers are in bloom now, a curtain call of daffodils nodding at passers-by. The few hyacinths I planted have blossomed, and the tulips will be next. But my yard doesn't look cared for. My flowers don't look well-tended.

Dandelions are sprouting in the beds and dead leaves and branches litter the lawn. Out back it is worse, a billion leaves caught between spreading yews, a billion leaves smothering whatever is struggling to emerge from the ground.

I walk down the street in search of more accomplished gardens, but most of them look like mine — not good, not bad, just there. But I keep walking and discover a few that make me pause. Not the huge, sprawling, perfectly manicured, lawn-service-tended lots, which are nice but impersonal, but the small, less dramatic gardens tended by people who, early in the morning or late at night, are outside,

plucking, pruning, picking, persevering; the gardens of people who take ordinary flowers and arrange them in an extraordinary way.

In one yard, daffodils surround the entire house, at least 100 of them standing tall and straight against the foundation like colorful extras in a Cecil B. De Mille movie. In another, the flowers are graduated like steps, tulips behind daffodils behind hyacinths.

In front of the Hellenic Nursing Home, a staid, brick building with a huge parking lot and a little lawn, more than 500 hyacinths in shades of purple and pink and blue sway like girls dressed up for a prom, and the sight is so unexpected, so startling, that I am overwhelmed by it.

Why am I going on about flowers? Because I admire the people who plant them. Why do they go through the effort of digging and watering and weeding and feeding and weeding and edging and watering again and again and again? Why do they work in the cold, in the dark, in the heat, in the rain? For the sole purpose of producing a flower that can be trampled by animals, plucked by people, devoured by insects, pummeled by rain, sheared by wind, withered by heat or frozen by cold?

For something that, even when it does survive, lives for two, maybe three weeks?

No. Gardeners plant flowers to feed their souls. The bonus is that when their gardens bloom, our souls are fed, too.

Molly

I didn't expect this. I didn't expect love at first sight followed by happily ever after. I was only being a good sport, going along for the ride, reneging on my years of "NO! NO! NO!" in order to make my oldest daughter happy. Yes, she could get a dog, but there was no way that I was going to take care of the dog. I was happy with my cats. I didn't want any part of a creature that barked and drooled and jumped on people and wasn't smart enough to use a litter box. "You may have your dog," I told my daughter, "but I do not want to have to walk that dog or clean up after that dog or play with that dog or worry about that dog. This is your dog, do you understand? Y-O-U-R-S, not mine."

She understood just fine. I was the one who did not understand.

It made sense that I fell a little in love with her when we met. Who wouldn't? At six-weeks-old she was small and round and tottered on legs so new they had trouble holding the rest of her up. It was natural that my heart jumped a little as she waddled toward us, as my daughter picked her up and said, "She's the one."

But liking her and liking to take care of her were two different things. "You're the one who's going to have to walk her in the cold and the ice and the snow," I said.

"I know," my daughter murmured, hugging the small thing closer.

"And you're the one who's going to have to play with her and train her and read dog care books and take her to the vet's."

"I know, Mom, I know."

So what happened? Here the rules were all established, my responsibility abdicated and I went asking for trouble.

"I'll take the dog for a walk," it began, harmlessly enough.

"I'll play with her for a while. I'll stay home and watch her so you can go out. Besides, I'm in the middle of the most excellent dog training book."

The incredible thing is I didn't mind taking care of Molly. I actually wanted to. Before she came into our lives, I believed that people who had dogs were totally insane. Why on earth would anyone bother? Dogs bark for no reason at all, they have bad breath all the time, they smell like dogs, they look at you while you're eating, they sneeze, they burp, they drool, they lick your face and have accidents on the carpet and chase cats and chew furniture and beg to be inside when they're out, and outside when they're in. They shed, they're a home for ticks and you have to board them when you go away. Why would any rational person choose to put up with all this?

Why, indeed.

I never thought I would enjoy the sound of a bark, but all of a sudden the sounds coming out of Molly's mouth make me smile. Her bark's a yip when she's excited and throaty when she's serious and a definite "I'm so happy to see you" in the morning when I appear to let her out. As for her breath, it isn't bad at all, it's sweet. And the way she smells, a combination of dog and outdoors, makes me feel 10 again.

Molly doesn't burp or drool or have accidents on the rug, though maybe when she's old she will. But I have a feeling I won't mind so much then because, to tell the truth, I really wouldn't mind so much now. I've changed. She's changed me. I read dog books instead of novels, ("Dog Tales" by Ray McSoley and The Monks of New Skete's "How To Be Your Dog's Best Friend" are my favorites) I initiate conversations with dog owners (mostly in the dog food aisle at the supermarket) and I browse these days in pet stores (Molly likes doggie bagels and rawhide bones).

I do all these things not because I have to — she is, after all, my daughter's dog — but incredibly, amazingly, because I want to.

Sweeter Than Chocolate

We eat the eggs — chocolate-covered marshmallow eggs — two weeks before Easter, in the middle of the fourth week of Lent. They are not Russell Stover or Fanny Farmer eggs and I assume that is why the chocolate tastes grainy and the marshmallow is bland.

"I think they taste delicious," my daughter says, reaching for her third. I try another and still there is nothing of the taste I remember.

How did I expect that there would be? The taste I recall wasn't just chocolate and sugar. It was a blend of sweets, yes, but combined with imminent spring, a child's faith, supreme sacrifice and the promise of eternal salvation.

It wasn't my salvation that was the promise. If it had been my soul at risk, I would not have given up ALL candy and ALL sweets on ALL the days of Lent, even Sundays when some of the kids indulged. Their teacher, a lay teacher, said Sundays didn't count.

And so after church they would head straight to Gilroy's and stuff their pockets with Hershey bars, Three Musketeers, Snickers and Squirrels and eat these all day from before lunch until well into the night. I, too, would have eaten candy on Sunday and have accepted the word of a lay teacher if Sister hadn't told us something extraordinary.

Jesus didn't break His fast on Sunday, Sister said. And Jesus didn't give up something frivolous, like candy. He gave up food. He gave up sustenance. He suffered great hunger. And He did this for us. Now we had the opportunity to do something for someone else.

Then she told us the wonderful thing: Sister said that if we gave up something we loved and never once cheated, if we abstained from whatever it was throughout Lent, then on Easter morning one poor soul stuck in the fires of Purgatory would be set free because of our sacrifice. A soul would meet God because of us.

What an incredible feeling of power to be able to free a soul. But what an incredible responsibility, too. One tiny M&M suddenly meant the difference between a soul's bliss and a soul's suffering.

Despite what was at stake, it was not easy abstaining from sweets. Sweets were everywhere. The stores were filled with the best things: pink marshmallow chicks, solid milk-chocolate bunnies, jelly beans, and my all-time favorite, chocolate-covered marshmallow eggs.

I don't know why I liked these the best, but I did.

Mongrel eggs, too, not even the expensive kind. Every Lent, I would buy a carton at the five-and-ten and keep them in my bedroom, in anticipation of Easter morning.

For the first few weeks I was happy just knowing they were there. But somewhere into the third or fourth week, I would break the seal, open the box and inhale, and as Easter grew closer I would spend more and more time drinking in their smell, looking at these things and dreaming of Easter morning when both an anonymous soul and I would be set free.

The richness of that chocolate has mingled over time with the sweetness of the wind that blew in under the sill of a drafty window. Spring and chocolate ever entwined, the fragrance of eternal life.

Easter eve, at the stroke of midnight, as the clock's hands became one, I was sure the soul, whom I now thought of as my soul, a sin of pride, became one with God, too. How many other souls became one with God at this moment? In the stillness of the night, I was certain I heard a chorus of them rejoicing in the wind.

After Mass on Easter morning, I could finally taste the chocolate I had coveted for weeks. Dressed in my Easter outfit, I would take a gloved hand and select first one egg then another. Gluttony after weeks of deprivation. A reward after sacrifice. Nothing has ever tasted so sweet.

Today my daughter asks why I am not eating the eggs. "I thought they were your favorite, Mom."

They were. But without sacrifice and salvation, they taste remarkably bland.

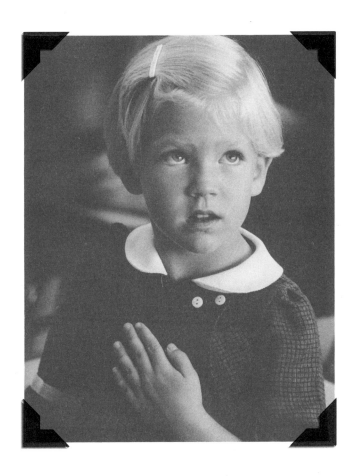

Spring Fever

It arrives every year, nestled in the buds of the forsythia, carried in an April breeze, coaxed to life by a series of sunny days: spring fever, that seasonal yearning for something just out of sight, something already past or too far in the distance, something only dreamed about, a thing as sweet as the scent of lilac and as fleeting as spring itself.

Spring fever. The first time I felt its warmth I didn't even know its name. I was a child sitting by an open window reading a book about people older than I, two teenagers newly in love. The teenagers were in a parked car, holding hands. A soft breeze ruffled the thin white curtains in the room where I read and carried the scent of rich earth into that room. And the heady fragrance — of night, of earth, of spring — became so intertwined with budding love that forever after the smell of April would bring with it the distant memory of two people I never knew, and a longing for something that never was.

All my life, spring fever has brought with it this yearning. I remember being 14, standing in the kitchen, the screen door open wide, ironing my father's shirts, an April breeze wafting in, wishing the shirts were someone else's, the man of my dreams, the man I would someday love.

I remember another spring, years later, actually getting my wish and ironing shirts for the man I love and still wishing for something else, wishing I were in Colorado on a mountaintop, or up in Maine walking along a beach.

I remember countless springs when all around me the world brimmed with color and light; when gardens grew overnight and magnolias sweetened the air and stoops were scrubbed and yards were raked and children appeared in pastels — in carriages, on skateboards, riding bicycles; when the world truly dazzled.

And still I ached for more.

Aching for more is the essence of spring fever. Shut indoors for months, layered under cottons and wools, our bodies yearn to shed not just these physical trappings of winter, but the psychological ones, as well.

And so, as the earth softens, so does our firm resolve to be hard-working, no-nonsense, dependable people. We pine for pleasure. We long to be free. All around us life blooms; the world beckons. And we want to play. Yet here we are stuck in the same place, burdened by the same problems, going through the same motions day after day after day.

I see the longing for more, for something better, for something *else* in people's eyes, the wish they could change, go somewhere new and start over. What's it all about, spring makes us ask? Why am I working? What am I working toward? What is the point of all this craziness? I want to get in a car and drive until the road stops. I want to walk along a beach until I can't walk anymore. I want to be 18 again. I want to do what I want to do. This is what most of us think.

The things we love, the possessions we prize, all our earthly treasures weigh us down like baggage in April; our worlds become burdens.

"I'm just tired," a friend says. "I'm tired of working two jobs. I'm tired of being responsible. I'm tired of being tired. Is this all there is?"

This is spring fever. In November, his soul is sheltered from its yearning and its needs, and slumbers within him as the seeds that will be flowers in spring sleep within the ground. His dreams are dormant then.

But now his soul, as are all our souls, is like the new life that is pushing up all over the ground, shedding darkness.

And if this process hurts a little — by making us look around, by forcing us to appraise our lives and notice where

we are and where we want to be, by causing us to yearn —
how different can it be from the hurt the young seedling must
feel as it forces its way through indifferent ground?

To grow takes strength. To reach for the unknown takes
courage. To live, and not merely exist, takes thought.

Enjoy, spring whispers. Slow down. Breathe in the air. Feel
the feelings. Savor the sun. Bask in the promise. Fall in love
with life.

And yearn. Follow your dreams. Listen to your heart. Get
in touch with your soul. It's spring. It's the only time you can.